IMAGES
of America

LANSING

CITY ON THE GRAND

1836–1939

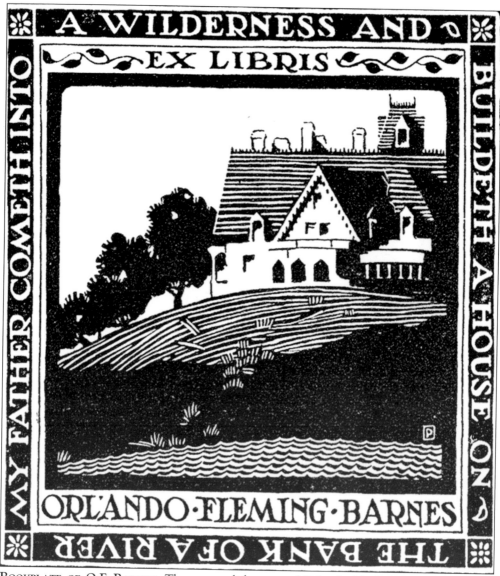

BOOKPLATE OF O.F. BARNES. The accomplishments of Orlando Mack Barnes and his son, Orlando Fleming Barnes, were instrumental to the development of Lansing. Both served Lansing as mayor. A lifelong interest of O.M. Barnes was his library, stated to be one of the finest in Michigan. Thus it is only proper to begin this volume with a bookplate from the library of O.F. Barnes honoring his father's pioneering spirit and their homestead, the Barnes mansion.

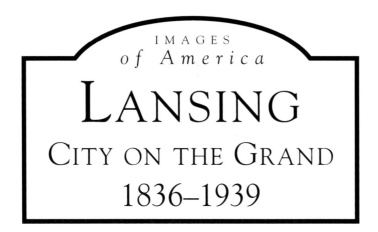

IMAGES
of America

LANSING
CITY ON THE GRAND
1836–1939

James MacLean and Craig A. Whitford

ARCADIA

Published by Arcadia Publishing,
an imprint of Tempus Publishing, Inc.
Charleston SC, Chicago, Portsmouth NH,
San Francisco

Printed in Great Britain.

Library of Congress Catalog Card Number: 2003110389

For all general information contact Arcadia Publishing at:
Telephone 843-853-2070
Fax 843-853-0044
E-Mail sales@arcadiapublishing.com
For customer service and orders:
Toll-Free 1-888-313-2665

Visit us on the internet at http://www.arcadiapublishing.com

To my parents, John and Elizabeth

To my wife Kathy and our children, Jon, Katie, Lisa, Dan, Jess, Beth, and Tim

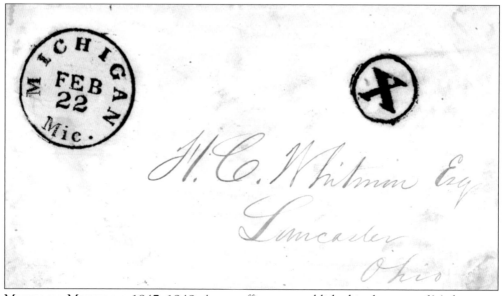

MICHIGAN, MICHIGAN, 1847–1848. A post office was established in the town of Michigan on April 27, 1847. George Washington Peck, Speaker of the House of Representatives, was appointed as the first postmaster. This envelope features a rare black circular date postmark, applied to outgoing letters during the short period in which Michigan, Michigan, existed. "Michigan" became Lansing on April 3, 1848.

CONTENTS

ACKNOWLEDGMENTS

The authors would like to thank the Forest Parke Memorial Library/Capital Area District Library (FPML/CADL), Barbara Caterino, the David R. Caterino Collection/Capital Area District Library (Caterino/CADL), the Historical Society of Greater Lansing (HSGL), Pat Heyden and the Lansing Police Department (LPD Historical File), "Babe" Weyant Ruth, Whitney Miller, and the MSU Archives and Historical Collection, for providing some of the photographs that appear in this book. Photographs that are not identified are the property of the authors.

The authors would also like to thank Anne Donohue and Jerry Lawler for their support and assistance throughout this project.

Finally, the reader should know that the authors have agreed to donate their royalties from this work to the Capital Area District Library and the Historical Society of Greater Lansing for continued support of local history.

INTRODUCTION

This photographic record about Lansing, city on the Grand and the capital of Michigan, focuses on the time period from 1836 through 1939. Located at the convergence of the Grand and Red Cedar Rivers, the city owes its existence to the legislative (or political) process. When Michigan was admitted to the Union in January, 1837, the adopted state constitution required that, "The seat of government for this state shall be Detroit, or at such place or places as may be prescribed by law, until the year eighteen hundred and forty-seven, when it shall be permanently located by the Legislature."

In 1847 the state legislature began their work of finding a permanent location as mandated by the state constitution. After much political debate the capital was permanently located within Lansing Township, Ingham County, with the name of the new capital city being Michigan. The legislature of 1848, before adjourning, renamed the capital Lansing.

In 1836, 11 years before locating the capital in the midst of a "dense forest," brothers Jerry and William Ford platted the town of "Biddle City." Located south of the Grand and Red Cedar Rivers, this paper city of 48 full blocks and 17 fractional ones was also provided with a "public square," a "church square," and an "academy square." Numerous lots were sold, but the plat was eventually abandoned and Biddle City faded into history.

During 1843, Col. John W. Burchard would build the first house in an area now known as North Lansing. Soon a small dam would be erected to harness the power of the Grand River for the use of a saw mill.

While Lansing may owe its existence to the political process, it is the pioneering entrepreneurs that have placed Lansing on the map. In August, 1897, inventor Ransom E. Olds founded the Olds Motor Vehicle Company, the first automobile company organized in Michigan. The growth, innovation, and prosperity of the automobile industry and her people have brought Lansing the honor of being called "The Automobile Capital."

In May, 1857, the first land grant college, the Michigan Agricultural College, was dedicated east of the city. Today, this same college, now called Michigan State University, is a world-class institution for higher education. During 1859, Lansing incorporated as a city with a population of just over 3,000. Today, Lansing boasts a population of more than 125,000.

This book captures the visual record of a growing and dynamic capital city from its beginning to just before the Second World War. Included are many rare and seldom seen images of Lansing's people, street scenes, businesses, manufacturing, schools, theatres, parades, maps, the police and fire departments, the state capitol, as well as the automobile industry and her product. Many of the photographs reproduced here are from the wonderful collection of the

Forest Parke Memorial Library of Local History housed in the Main Library of the Capital Area District Library in downtown Lansing. Images from the collections of David R. Caterino, J.P. Edmonds, and photographer Charles H. Mead are included. Additional images have been provided by a number of local residents and historians for inclusion in this work.

By publishing *Lansing: City on the Grand*, the images, along with their descriptions, will be preserved for future generations to enjoy.

The members and Board of the Historical Society of Greater Lansing continue to preserve and promote the history of the capital city and the surrounding community.

One
CITY VIEWS

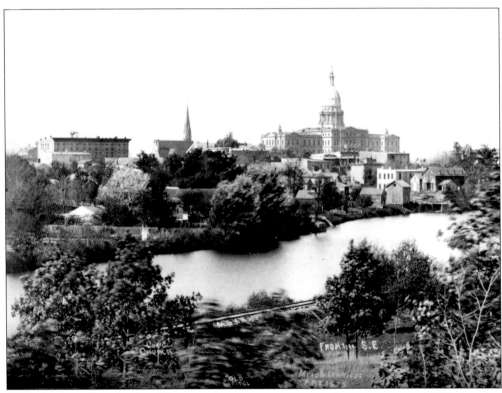

A BEAUTIFUL BIRD'S EYE VIEW OF LANSING FROM THE SOUTHEAST, c. 1879. Lansing artist and photographer Charles H. Mead captures a unique view of the growing city. In between the Lansing House on the far left and the Capitol on the right, the steeple of the Plymouth Congregational Church and the cupola of the old capitol are clearly visible. This image shows the beauty and breadth of the Grand River with the Michigan Southern Railroad tracks running parallel. (HSGL.)

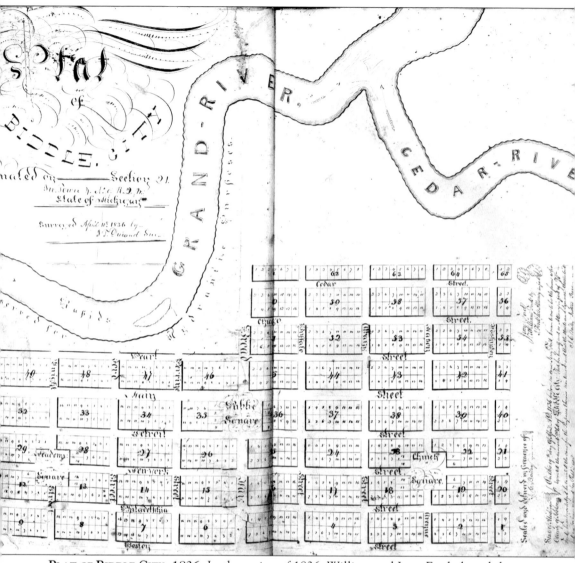

PLAT OF BIDDLE CITY, 1836. In the spring of 1836, William and Jerry Ford platted the town of Biddle City, named in honor of Major John Biddle, who served with distinction in the war of 1812 and was later a member and president of the state Constitutional Convention. This "paper city," located south of the Grand and Red Cedar Rivers, comprised almost all the south half of section 21. Large spaces were provided for a "Public Square," "Academy Square," and a "Church Square." Many lots were sold, but not a soul occupied Biddle City.

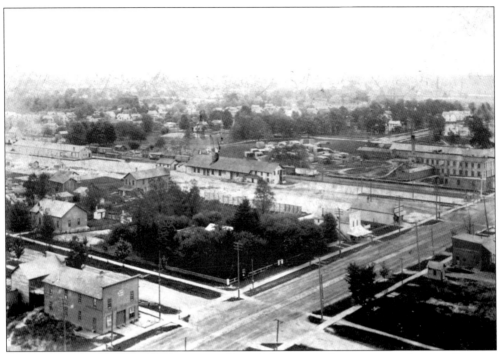

AN EARLY VIEW OF THE CORNER OF EAST MICHIGAN AVENUE AND LARCH STREET. Heading north on Larch Street, which runs from the bottom right to left, the first building on the east side of Larch is the old Larch Street School (Fifth Ward). It was later used as the first Pilgrim Congregational Church, which was responsible for moving the building to this location. In the center of the photograph along the railroad tracks is what is believed to be the old Union Station. This is difficult to verify because no other images of the station survive. Further along Michigan Avenue, the Crystal Creamery is the two-story building to the right in the photograph. (FPML/CADL.)

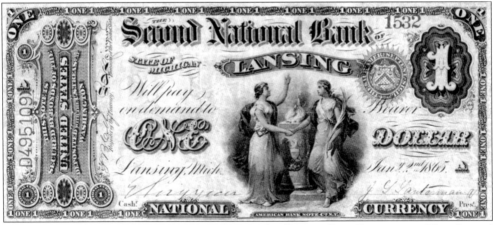

THE SECOND NATIONAL BANK OF LANSING, $1 LARGE SIZE BANKNOTE. The Second National Bank issued $202,900 worth of $1, $5, $50, and $100 banknotes from 1864 through 1884, when the bank became Longyear's Bank. This rare $1 original series banknote carries the pen signatures of Ephraim Longyear, Cashier, and Jacob L. Lanterman, Vice President, and was issued between 1864 and 1875. Only three of these $1 notes are known to exist.

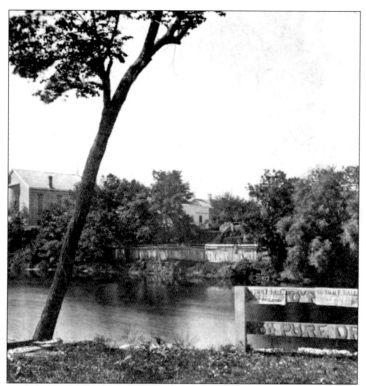

A View of the Grand River Looking Southwest from the East Bank. Visible in the photograph is the Universalist Church, which was dedicated in 1863. What is remarkable about this image is the total lack of industry on the river at this point. In time, a tremendous amount of industry developed on both banks further north along the river. The placards on the fence state "Go to the B.F. Hall," which is ironic because B.F. Hall was the photographer who took this picture. (FPML/CADL.)

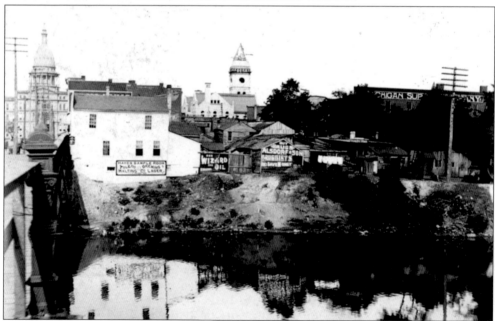

Looking West along Michigan Avenue in 1895. In the distance you can see not only the Capitol but also the clock tower of old city hall. The tower at this phase is under construction and the clock and roof are not yet in place. The white building, Hayes Sample Room, a purveyor of Wine, Liquor and Cigars, would later become the site of the Hotel Wentworth. Behind that, where the shacks are, is where the ill-fated Hotel Kerns would be built. (FPML/CADL.)

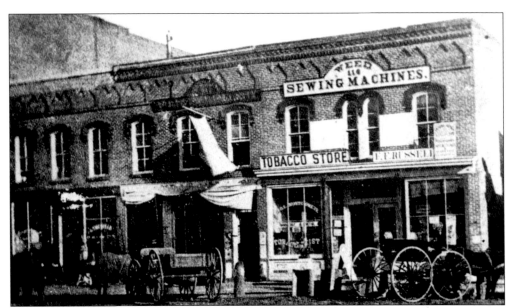

THE CENTRAL BUSINESS DISTRICT, c. 1870s. In 1871 Franklin F. Russell opened his book and stationary store at what is known today as 117 South Washington Avenue. Born in Walpole, New Hampshire, in 1820, Russell moved to Lansing in 1856 and began working in the book and stationary store of A.J. Viele. When Mr. Viele later left Lansing, F.F. Russell acquired the business. Due to poor health, F.F. Russell was forced to sell the business in 1896 to Orin A. Jenison. Russell died in 1900 and was mourned by all. Next door to the Russell Bookstore is Montgomery Tobacco. It was operated by Charles Kerr, son of John A. Kerr, the former publisher of the *State Republican*. The streets are still unpaved at this point and there seem to be only wooden planks for sidewalks. (FPML/CADL.)

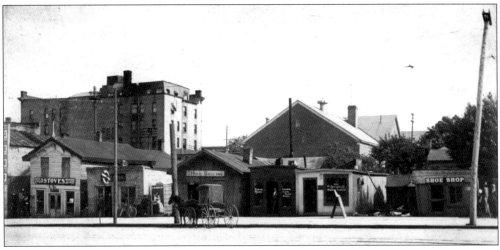

THE SOUTH SIDE OF WEST MICHIGAN AVENUE BETWEEN CAPITOL AND WASHINGTON AVENUES, 1890s. The large building to the left in the background is the Hollister Building and just to the right in the background is the rear of the Elks' home. This block was always an eyesore and an embarrassment for the city fathers. The block was later razed and the Oakland Building was constructed on this location, only to be destroyed by fire in 1923. The Romney Building is today located on this site. (FPML/CADL.)

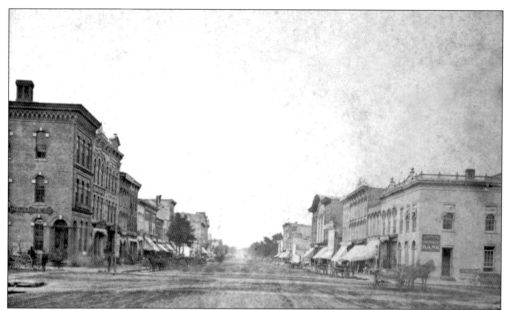

WASHINGTON AVENUE NORTH FROM MICHIGAN AVENUE, C. 1870S. Looking north from Michigan Avenue, the Second National Bank building is on the right. A short distance away is one of Lansing's first theaters, Mead's Hall, easily identified by its hump-back roof structure. On the left is a boot sign marking the shoe store of H.A. Woodworth with the ornate roof of Buck's Opera House visible in the distance. Photo by J.H. Scotford.

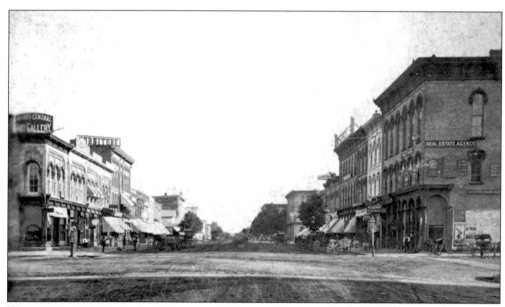

WASHINGTON AVENUE SOUTH FROM MICHIGAN AVENUE, C. 1870S. Looking south from Michigan Avenue, Woods Central Art Gallery is on the northwest corner above the Lansing National Bank offices; the "Big Book Store" of F.F. Russell, Baker & Porter Furniture, and the Glove & Mitten Factory of John A. Elder & Co. are all depicted on the left. On the right and starting at the corner are the real estate offices of Jones & Porter, watchmaker H.B. Morgan, and Ingersoll's Dry Goods Store. Photo by J.H. Scotford.

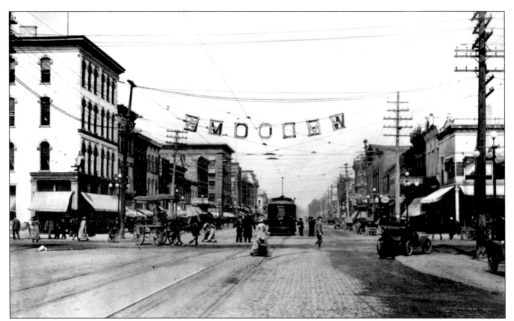

WASHINGTON AVENUE NORTH FROM MICHIGAN AVENUE, c. 1910S. Compare this view looking north from Michigan Avenue with the one on the opposite page and the changes of nearly 40 years are dramatic. Horse-drawn wagons share the brick-paved city streets with the automobile and streetcars. The boot sign of H.A. Woodworth still marks the merchant's location and Buck's Opera House is now known as Baird's Opera House, operated by Fred J. Williams and Frank J. Stahl. (FPML/CADL.)

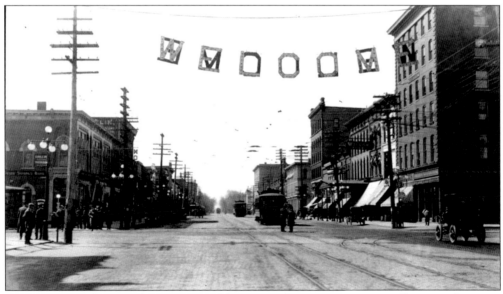

WASHINGTON AVENUE SOUTH FROM MICHIGAN AVENUE, c. 1910S. Compare this view looking south from Michigan Avenue with the one on the opposite page. The building on the right, the Prudden Block, home of the American Savings Bank, has replaced its 1870s counterpart. Electric wires power not only the modern streetcars and street lamps but also the lighted overhead WELCOME banner and the merchant signs. (FPML/CADL.)

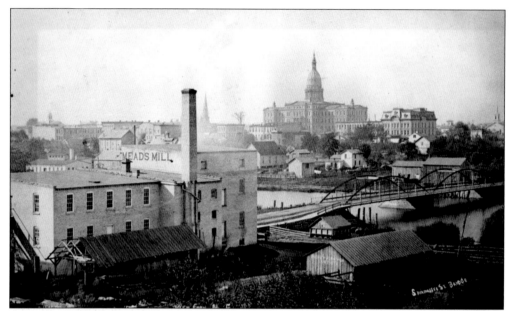

BIRD'S EYE VIEW OF LANSING LOOKING SOUTHWEST, C. 1879. This marvelous view by Mead & Jennings, Artists, shows the newly completed capitol building rising above the cityscape. To the right is Buck's Opera House. In the foreground is the Shiawassee Street Bridge and Mead's Mill. To the left and in the distance is the faint image of the first capitol building in Lansing. (HSGL.)

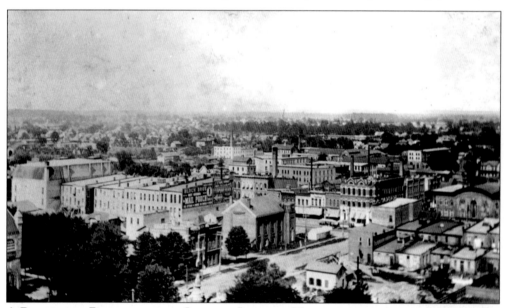

A PANORAMIC PHOTOGRAPH OF LANSING LOOKING NORTHEAST FROM THE CAPITOL. The back of the majestic Gladmer Theater can be seen on the left; at the time of this photograph it was known as the Baird's Opera House. On the northwest corner of Washington Avenue and Ottawa Street is the Central Methodist Episcopal Church, which was built in 1862 and stood until the early 1900s. One of the interesting aspects of this church is that the belfry was never completed. This photograph shows the vibrant nature of Lansing just before the beginning of the twentieth century. (FPML/CADL.)

16

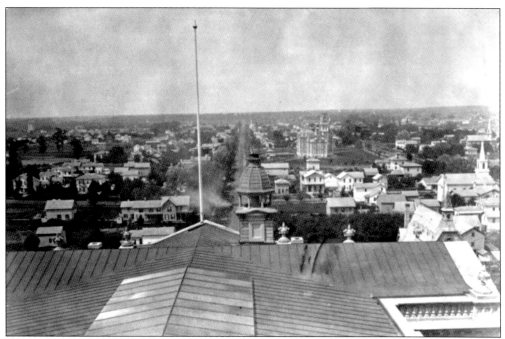

LOOKING NORTH FROM THE CAPITOL, C. 1879. On the far left is St. Mary's (Catholic) Church at the corner of Madison and Chestnut. Just left of the flag pole is the residence of W.S. George, State Printer and Publisher of the Lansing Republican. To the right is the Lansing High School, built during 1874–75. In the lower right corner is St. Paul's (Protestant Episcopal) Church, then the Baptist Church, on the corner of Capitol and Ionia, and at the far right is the First Presbyterian Church on the corner of Washington Avenue and Genesee Street. Photo by C.H. Mead. (HSGL.)

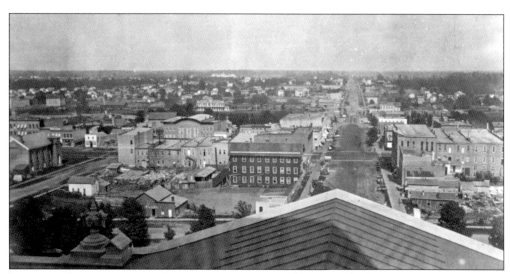

LOOKING EAST FROM THE CAPITOL, C. 1879. In this scene looking east down Michigan Avenue, the growing heart of the city is in full view. The present-day City Hall will one day be built on the vacant lot to the left. The hump-back roof of Mead's Hall is visible, and above it lies the Lake Shore and Michigan Southern Railroad Depot, located on the east bank of the Grand River. Photo by C.H. Mead. (HSGL.)

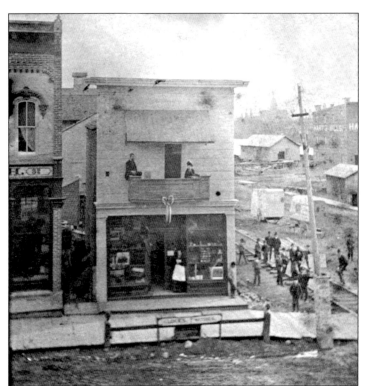

AN INTERESTING VIEW OF NORTH LANSING LOOKING SOUTHWEST. In the background the new State Capitol can be seen, and it is interesting to notice that the Capitol seems to be elevated. To the right is Hart's Flour Mill, which was expanded in 1875 at a cost of $14,000. The mill would be destroyed by fire on September 26, 1877 and rebuilt by Arthur Hart in 1878, only on a much smaller scale. The railroad tracks just to the left of the building are for the Lake Shore and Michigan Southern Railroad. (FPML/CADL.)

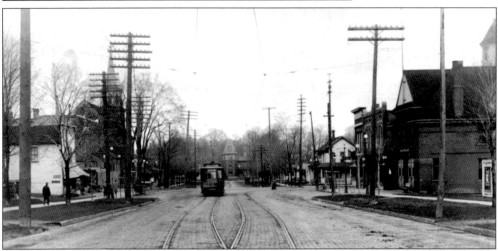

LOOKING NORTH ALONG WASHINGTON AVENUE FROM MAPLE STREET c. 1910. The streetcar is about to make a right turn onto Franklin Avenue, now Grand River. On the right of the photograph, the brick building with the two large doors is Lansing Fire Station No. 2. On the left of the photograph, the spire of the Franklin Avenue Presbyterian Church is visible. On the southwest corner of Washington and Franklin Avenue was the Walker Block, built in 1909 and just visible in the photograph. It was the home of Walker Grocerataria and George Daschner Meat Market. Dr. R.J. Lange had an office on the second floor. The small clapboard building with the awning to the left in the photograph was the Eldorado Fruit & Tobacco store at 1133 North Washington, which specialized in serving the needs of Lansing's Italian community. (FPML/CADL.)

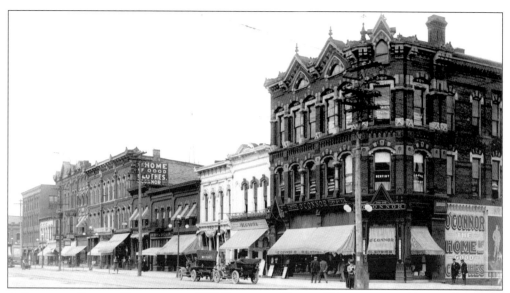

A STRIKING STREET VIEW OF THE 200 BLOCK OF NORTH WASHINGTON AVENUE LOOKING NORTH FROM OTTAWA STREET. The beautiful building on the corner was the men's clothing shop of James O'Connor, "Home of good clothes O'Connor," next door was the Theatorium, a theater and sometime vaudeville house, which would later become the Empress, owned by James M. Neal. This image helps to demonstrate how important the central business district was to Lansing. (FPML/CADL.)

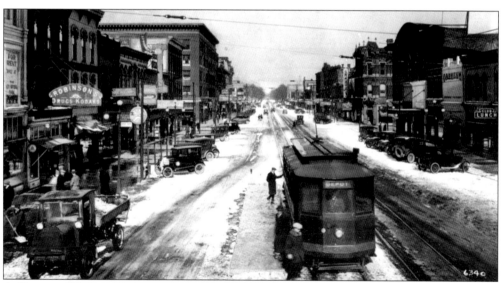

A VIEW OF WASHINGTON AVENUE LOOKING NORTH FROM MICHIGAN AVENUE IN 1922. As in previous photographs, the importance of the streetcar to the transportation needs of the public is obvious. What is interesting is the increased number of automobiles visible in this photograph. The building with the hump back roofline to the right is Mead's Hall. The hall was built by James Mead sometime between 1862 and 1865. When Mark Twain was scheduled to speak at Mead's Hall, he was taken for a coach ride through the unpaved streets of Lansing. When one of his hosts pointed to the width of Lansing's streets, Twain is said to have quipped "Yes, they are about as wide as they are deep." Mead's Hall was torn down in 1971. (FPML/CADL.)

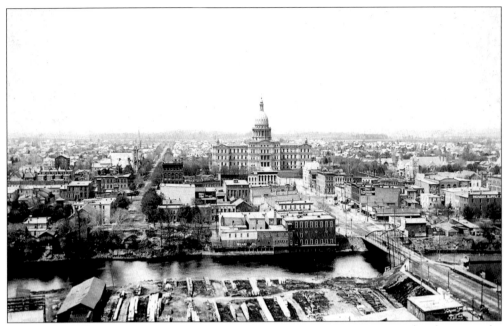

STANDPIPE VIEW OF LANSING LOOKING WEST, C. 1890S. A popular location for photographers to capture the city was the standpipe located on south Cedar Street. This view was taken prior to the construction of a new wide steel bridge on Michigan Avenue, crossing the Grand River. (FPML/CADL.)

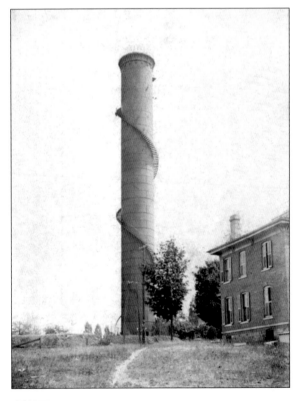

THE MYSTERIOUS STANDPIPE, C. 1890S. The aforementioned standpipe was constructed in 1885 and served as the city's storage tank for water. The tower was located east of Cedar Street and south of Michigan Avenue, where the Board of Water and Light have their holding tanks today. The remarkable aspect of the standpipe was that you could walk to the top on the circular staircase that wraps around the tower. Many a photographer took advantage of this and quite a few panoramic photographs were taken. The standpipe was torn down in 1949. (FPML/CADL.)

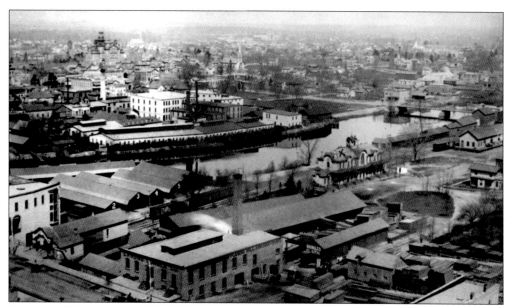

LOOKING NORTHWEST FROM THE STANDPIPE. In the distance is Lansing High School, as well as the Michigan School for the Blind, which is slightly less visible. The Bement factory is the long single story building on the west bank of the Grand River, and where the factory ends, the white two-story building built right up to the edge of the river is the clubhouse of the Grand River Boat Club. The clubhouse actually stood in the center of East Ottawa as it ended at the Grand River. Marked with an X in the center of the photograph on the east bank is the old Lake Shore and Michigan Southern Railroad Station. The station was built in 1868 and razed in 1938. (FPML/CADL.)

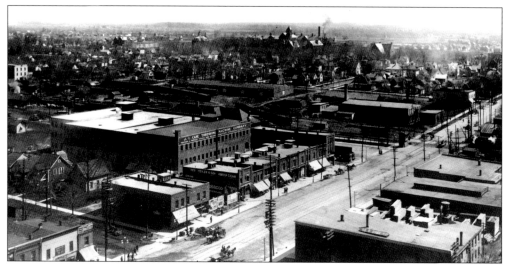

A PANORAMIC PHOTOGRAPH FROM THE STANDPIPE LOOKING NORTHEAST. Visible in the center and in the distance of this image is the State Industrial School for Boys located at Pennsylvania Avenue and Shiawasee Street. The city water trucks are near the bottom of the image proceeding east on Michigan Avenue, and are wetting down the road in an effort to control the dust that was kicked up on the unpaved streets. Barely visible is the roof of the Union Railroad Depot, just above the J.I. Case Threshing Machine Company. (FPML/CADL.)

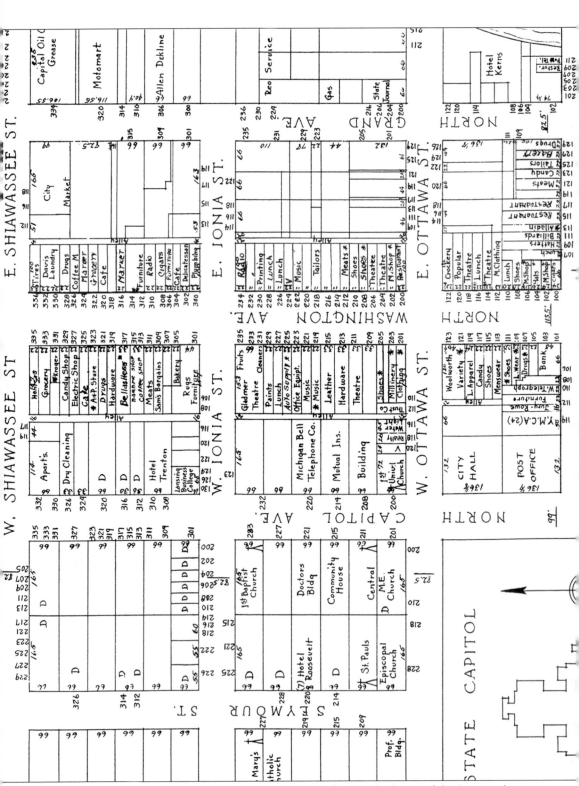

MAP OF DOWNTOWN LANSING, C. 1929. This map depicts the heart of the Lansing business

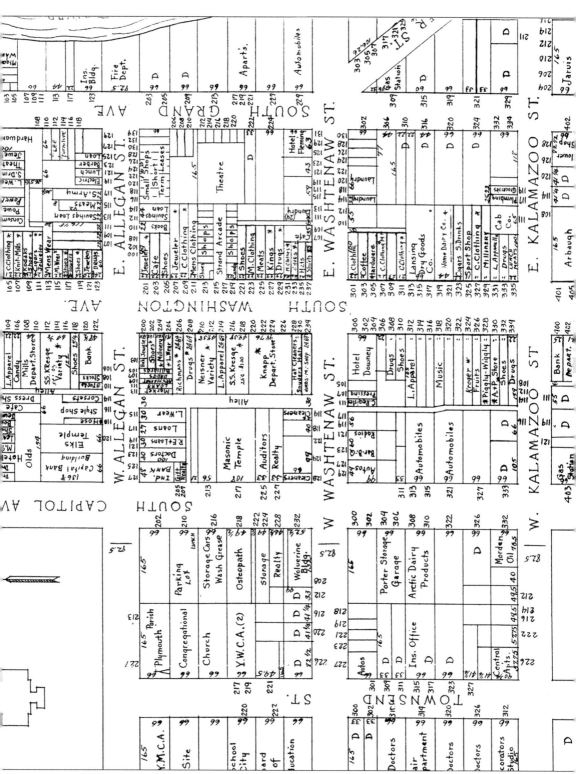

district on the eve of the Great Depression.

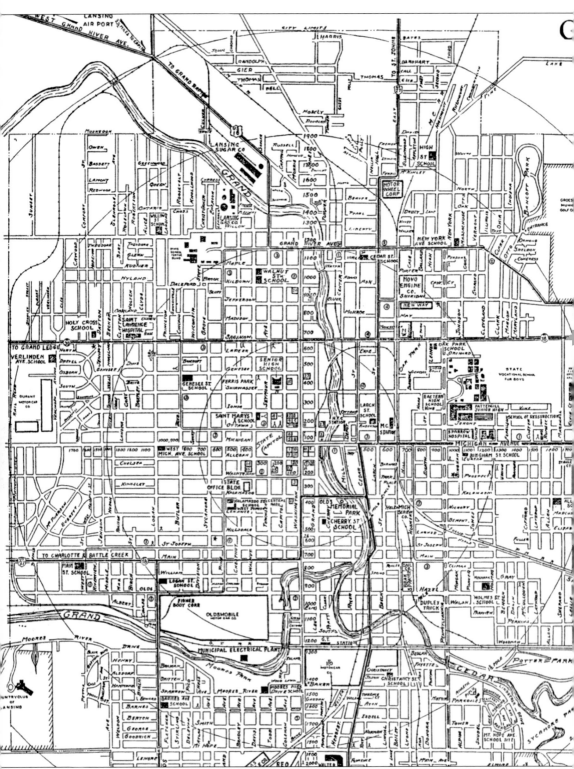

GREATER LANSING AND EAST LANSING MAP, 1929.

24

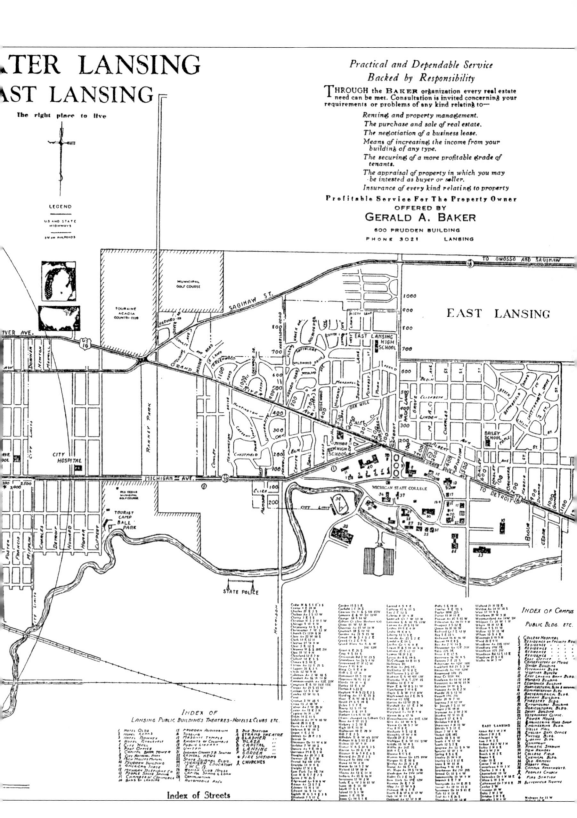

ATER LANSING
AST LANSING

The right place to live

EAST LANSING

LEGEND

U.S AND STATE HIGHWAYS

S W AM RAILROADS

MICHIGAN STATE COLLEGE

INDEX OF CAMPUS
PUBLIC BLDG. ETC.

INDEX OF
LANSING PUBLIC BUILDINGS THEATRES HOTELS & CLUBS ETC.

Index of Streets

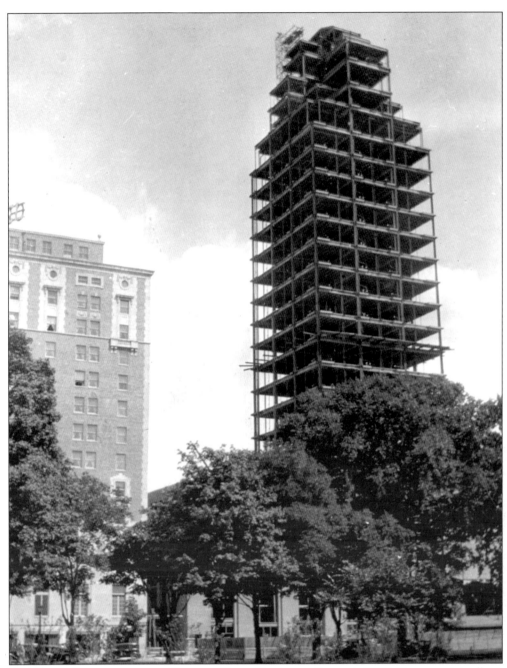

THE STEEL SKELETON OF THE CAPITAL BANK TOWER IN JULY OF 1930. Known originally as the Capital Bank Tower, this structure was 345 feet tall when completed, had 104,000 square feet of office space, used 3.5 millions pounds of structural steel, 654,000 bricks in 17 different colors, and had a sub-basement for parking. The tower has been named the Olds Tower and the Michigan National Tower. Oddly enough, in 1931 the first tenant was not the Capital National Bank, but rather Miller Bailey & Company, who first occupied their offices on January 15, 1931. The building was still not complete and the staff of Miller Bailey & Company had to use the construction lifts to get to their offices on the ninth floor. (FPML/CADL.)

Two

BUSINESS AND
INDUSTRY

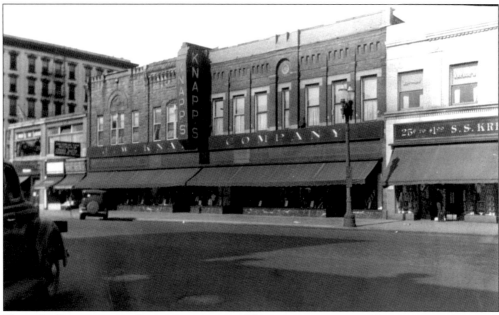

KNAPP'S DEPARTMENT STORE, C. 1930S. Three partners, Reynolds, Jewett, and Knapp, purchased N.F. Jenison Dry Goods Store at 123 North Washington Avenue and opened a retail store with 6,000 square feet of space on February 1, 1896. In 1908 the business incorporated as J.W. Knapp Company and moved to 220–226 South Washington Avenue. In 1928 the store was renovated and expanded at a cost of $15,000 in an attempt to compete with F.W. Arbaugh Company. This photograph shows the store's location at 220 South Washington Avenue, and to the left one can see the Hotel Downey before it was torn down and replaced with the new Knapp's building in 1936. (FPML/CADL.)

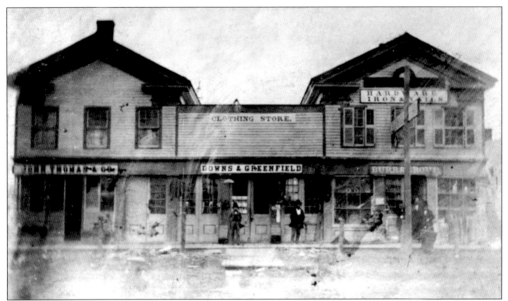

AN EARLY PHOTOGRAPH OF THE "BUSINESS DISTRICT" OF LANSING IN THE 1850s. The structure on the right is Burr & Grove Hardware, where their sign proclaims they sold iron and nails. It would later be replaced with a brick structure. In the center of the image is Downs & Greenfield Tailor and Clothing Shop, Downs being the first tailor in Lansing. On the left is the general store of John Thomas & Co. These shops furnished everything the residents of early Lansing could have desired. It would be interesting to see these entrepreneurs' reaction to a shopping mall. (FPML/CADL.)

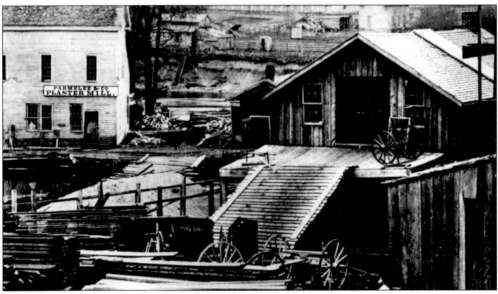

THE PARMALEE PLASTER MILL ON MILL STREET AND RACE. A plaster mill in the late 1800s did not produce plaster for construction or for business; rather it produced plaster, or plaister. Plaster or plaister was a finely ground gypsum used as a fertilizer for crops. The less expensive guano eventually replaced plaster as the fertilizer used by most farmers. The mill was destroyed by fire in 1866. (FPML/CADL.)

28

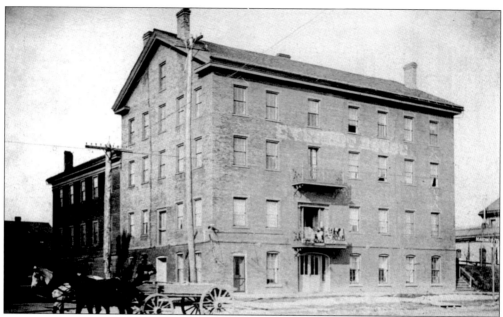

LANSING'S EARLIEST HOTEL. The Benton House, built in 1847 on the northwest corner of Washington Avenue and Main Street, later to be the site of the R.E. Olds Mansion, the Benton House was the first brick structure in Lansing. The hotel was owned by Charles P. Bush, John Thomas, and George W. Lee and was a favorite gathering place for state legislators. The Benton House eventually fell out of favor as new and centrally located hotels were built. The building was purchased in the 1860s and operated as a private school. It was subsequently operated as a hotel again in the 1870s and was renamed the Everett House. Its glory days well in the past, the Everett House was razed in 1902 and the Olds Mansion was erected in its place. (FPML/CADL.)

AN INVITATION TO THE NEW YEAR'S BALL TO BE HELD AT THE BENTON HOUSE IN 1851. The Benton House was the place in Lansing to be seen. The New Year's Ball was the event of the season and many citizens of Lansing turned out in their finery to participate in the celebration. (FPML/CADL.)

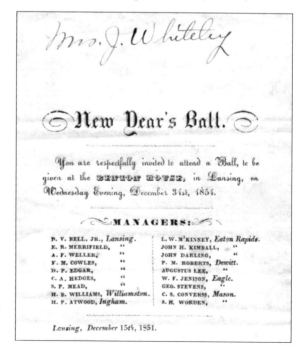

Mrs. J. Whitely

New Year's Ball.

You are respectfully invited to attend a Ball, to be given at the BENTON HOUSE, in Lansing, on Wednesday Evening, December 31st, 1851.

MANAGERS:

P. V. BELL, JR., *Lansing.*	L. W. M'KINSEY, *Eaton Rapids.*	
E. R. MERRIFIELD, "	JOHN H. KIMBALL, "	
A. F. WELLER, "	JOHN DARLING, "	
F. M. COWLES, "	P. M. ROBERTS, *Dewitt.*	
D. P. EDGAR, "	AUGUSTUS LEE, "	
C. A. HEDGES, "	W. F. JENISON, *Eagle.*	
S. F. MEAD, "	GEO. STEVENS, "	
H. B. WILLIAMS, *Williamston.*	C. S. CONVERSS, *Mason.*	
H. P. ATWOOD, *Ingham.*	S. H. WORDEN, "	

Lansing, December 15th, 1851.

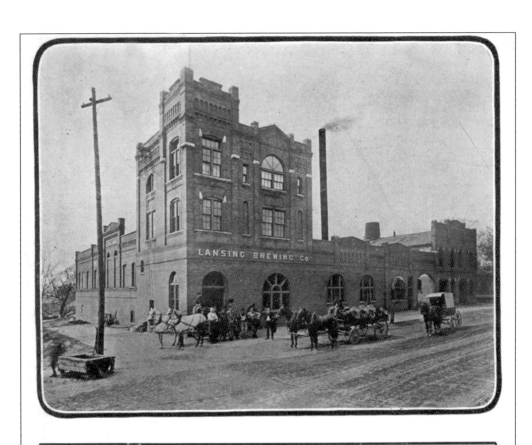

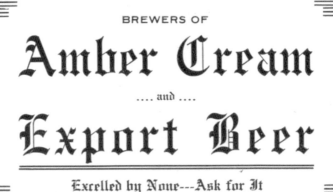

BREWERS OF

Amber Cream

.... and ....

Export Beer

Excelled by None---Ask for It

BOTTLED EXPRESSLY FOR FAMILY USE

Bell Phone 370   Citizens' Phone 571

LANSING BREWING COMPANY, 1906. This brewery operated between 1898 and 1914 in North Lansing at 1301 Turner. The brewery produced five types of beer: Amber Cream, Export, Bohemian, Lager, and Hofbrau. In 1906 the brewery's production capacity was 15,000 barrels a year.

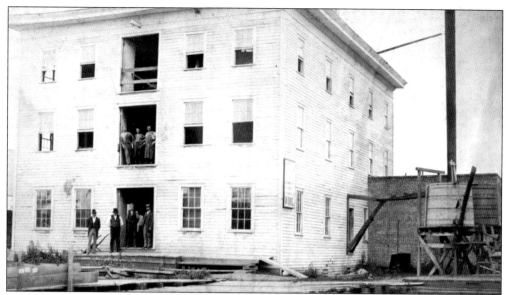

THE PARMALEE WOOLEN MILL. This mill once stood on the northeast corner of Franklin Avenue (Grand River) and Turner Street. The mill would have been located in North Lansing on the millrace, which has been backfilled and is now part of the River Trail. The mill burned on September 26, 1877. The fire started at four o'clock one afternoon and originated in the nearby Hart Milling Company. Both the Hart Mill and the Parmalee & Company Mill were destroyed. Losses were put at $83,000. This photograph has been identified as both the Parmalee Woolen Mill and the Carmer's Woolen Mill. This misidentification may just be a mistake because in 1878 the Carmer, Parmalee, and Capital Mills companies operated on Mill Street and were in business jointly until the mid 1880s. (FPML/CADL.)

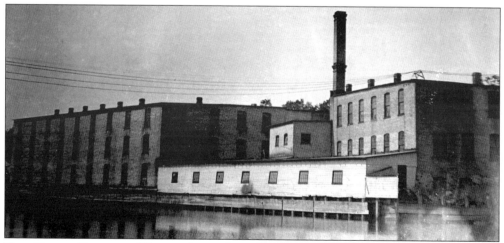

THE CLARK CARRIAGE WORKS. Located on the west bank of the Grand River near Grand and Kalamazoo, the Clark Carriage Works was one of the city of Lansing's oldest manufacturing businesses. Established by Albert Clark in 1865, the company flourished, producing fine carriages and wagons. At its peak the company employed 125 men in the factory and had five traveling salesmen. The vice president of the company was Frank G. Clark, later of Clarkmobile fame. On July 3, 1906, the 10,000-square foot factory was destroyed by fire, less than two years after the death of its founder, Albert Clark. (FPML/CADL.)

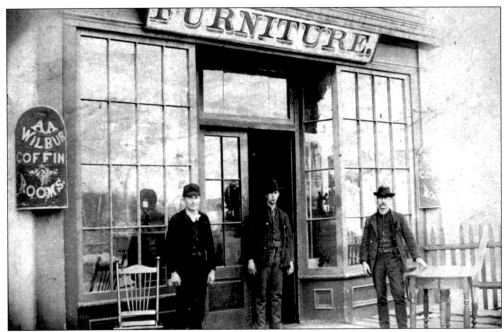

A.A. Wilbur Furniture Store. Located at the easternmost edge of the Franklin Avenue Bridge, the A.A. Wilbur Furniture Store was a fixture in North Lansing for many years. It is interesting to notice that not only did A.A. Wilbur sell furniture (some of his wares are visible in front of the building), but he also served as an undertaker and rented out rooms. The photograph is from 1896 and only Harvey McKeen standing to the right is identified. (FPML/CADL.)

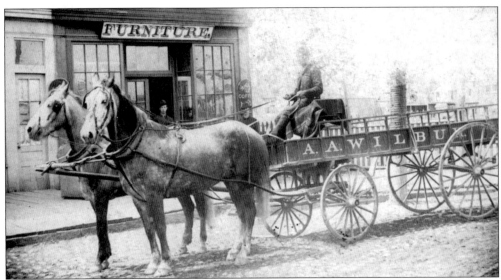

The Delivery Wagon for A.A. Wilbur Furniture Store. Mr. Wilbur learned the furniture trade by serving an apprenticeship with the Buck Furniture business and many of the pieces Wilbur sold at his store were built by Buck Furniture, located on the opposite side of the street. Mr. Wilbur was active in politics and served for many years as the city of Lansing's mortician. The men in the background are the same as those in the previous photograph; Harvey McKeen is in the center background. (FPML/CADL.)

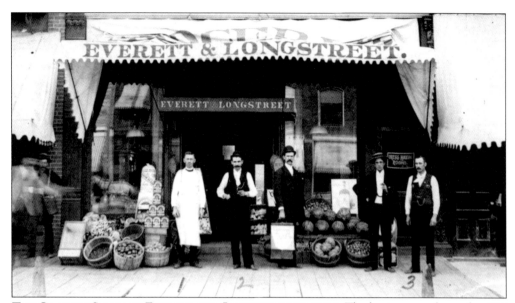

THE GROCERY STORE OF EVERETT AND LONGSTREET IN 1894. The business was located at 320 South Washington and only three of those present in the photograph are identified. If you look closely you can see numbers under some of the men; number one is Chet Leonard, the second is Charlie Longstreet, and number three is John Everett. By 1896 John Everett had left the business, which operated until 1901 or 1902. Charlie Longstreet's son Anson would later become president of Longstreet Lumber Company, and Charles would serve as it bookkeeper. (FPML/CADL.)

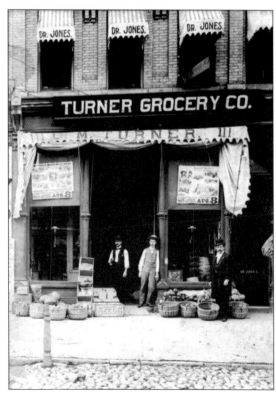

TURNER GROCERY STORE ON EAST MICHIGAN AVENUE IN 1896. Leaning against the door is J.A. Turner; his father stands in the center of the doorway and the dapper man wearing the derby is Dr. E. Jones, whose offices were on the second floor of the building. The banners in the windows are advertisements for "Buffalo Bill's Wild West and Congress of Rough Riders." These are not the same Rough Riders that fought in the Spanish American War; rather they were a group of international skilled horsemen who participated in the Wild West Show. (FPML/CADL.)

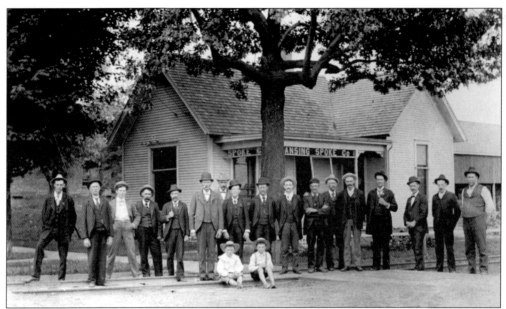

THE LANSING SPOKE COMPANY, FOUNDED IN 1891 BY E.S. PORTER AND GEORGE KNEAL.
The company produced wheel spokes, bent rims, and wagon hounds. The factory was destroyed by fire in September 1894 and quickly rebuilt with increased capacity; unfortunately, the company did not survive the advent of the automobile era. Only two men are identified in the photograph. Second from the left is Jasper J. Hayden and next to him is Charles H. Hayden, who later became a respected attorney in the Lansing area. (FPML/CADL.)

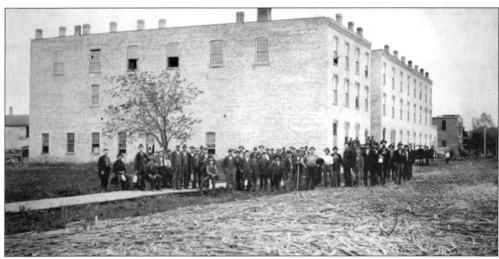

LANSING WAGON WORKS WAS ONE OF THE MANY WAGON AND COACHBUILDERS ACTIVE IN LANSING. Located at 504 North Grand Avenue just north of the Bement Factory, the Lansing Wagon Works was organized in 1881 and incorporated in 1887 with $120,000 in capital. The officers of the company in 1886 are names familiar to students of Lansing history: Fredrick Thoman, president; T.M. Cooley, vice president, E.F. Cooley, secretary and treasurer. Later in 1887, O.M. Barnes would become president of the company. By 1895 the Lansing Wagon Company was producing 5,000 vehicles a year with transfer houses in Rochester, New York, Baltimore, Maryland, and Kansas City, Missouri. (FPML/CADL.)

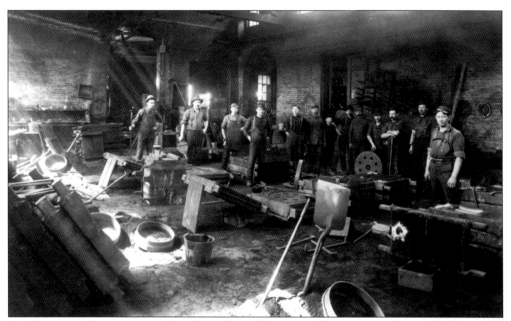

AN INTERIOR SHOT OF THE OLD GREY IRON FOUNDRY, PART OF THE LANSING IRON AND ENGINE WORKS, C. 1890. By today's standards, the working and safety conditions that existed at this time were appalling. The skill of these workmen helped to establish Lansing as a leader in the automotive and engine production fields. Of all the historical photographs of Lansing that exist, this one is a particular favorite. (FPML/CADL.)

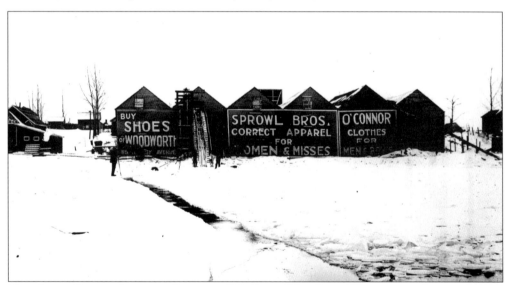

THE CLEAR-BAUER COMPANY CUTTING "UP RIVER" ICE JUST WEST OF THE LOGAN STREET BRIDGE IN 1917. Prior to the advent of the refrigerator, ice for the home was cut from local rivers and allowed for the storage of goods that would spoil if not kept cool. The conveyor for moving the ice from the river and into the storage sheds is visible in the center of the photograph. The ice was packed in sawdust and straw and lasted until September or October. Why was it called "up river" ice? Well, many people believed that prior to sewage treatment it was better to cut the ice up river of the city. The Pure Ice Company purchased the Clear-Bauer Company in 1920. (FPML/CADL.)

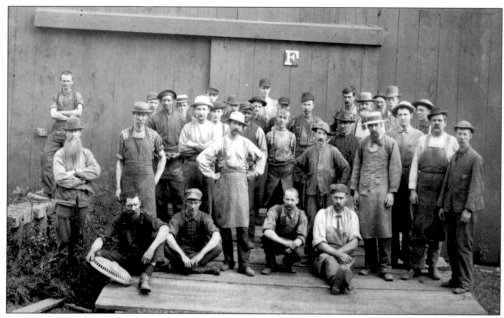

A Portrait of the Workmen at E. Bement and Sons, c. 1890s. Unfortunately, no one in the photograph is identified. The company employed 396 men and four women in a large factory at Grand River and Ionia Streets. Bement's was known for producing stoves that were well-built and reliable. Unfortunately, by 1907 the company failed in one of the many depressions that occurred in the period between 1890 and 1910. (FPML/CADL.)

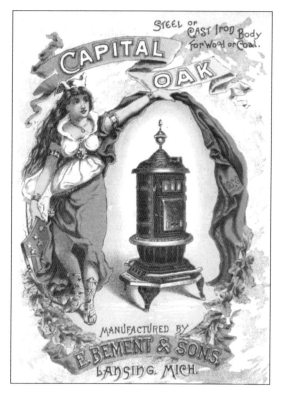

The Capitol Oak Stove #25 produced by Bement of Lansing, Michigan. A best-seller among Bement large stoves, the Capitol Oak was "For heating halls and large stores and other public places. There is no stove so effective and economical as the # 25 Capitol Oak. With two sheets of steel it makes it the largest oak stove on the market." The cost for this 90-inch-tall, 525-pound monster was $60.

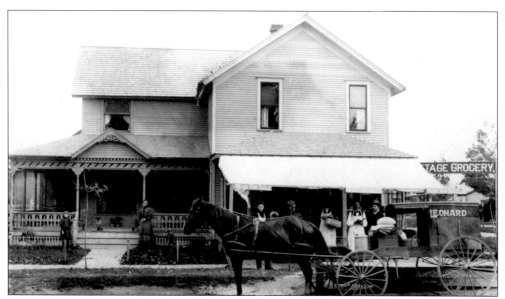

THE LEONARD COTTAGE GROCERY AT 333 SOUTH BUTLER. Chauncey B. Leonard was a grocer in Lansing for over 47 years and began working in the grocery business at the age of 13 for John Whitney. The people and the dog in the photograph are, from left to right, as follows: Iva May Leonard, Chauncey's dog Gippy on the porch, Emma Leonard (Chauncey's wife), Ora Bailey, Harry Flint, Chauncey Leonard, and Mr. Shamier. Chauncey Leonard would later move his business to 429 West Lenawee, and retire from the grocery business in 1920. (FPML/CADL.)

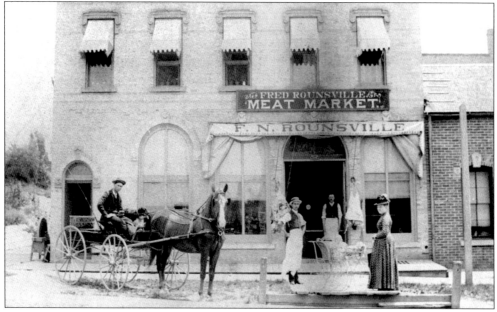

ROUNSVILLE MARKET, ESTABLISHED IN 1891 ON THE CORNER OF CEDAR AND MICHIGAN AVENUES. Fred N. Rounsville operated this market for ten years until starting J. Clear Company, later to be known as Rounsville Cartage, which he operated for 45 years. He was also associated with Jacob Sleight's Artificial Stone Company and was a director of the Duplex Truck Company. (FPML/CADL.)

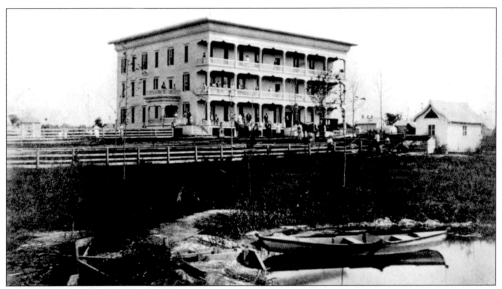

THE MINERAL WELL HOTEL AND SPA. Built in 1870, the hotel was where the wealthy sought the water cure for rheumatism, paralyses, diabetes, piles, liver complaints, kidney complaints, eruptions of the skin, weak lungs, inflamed eyes, chronic diarrhea, and the afflictions of the mucous membranes. Located on the east side of River Street, the hotel had 25 bathrooms, facilities for hot and cold showers, a vapor mineral bath, and a plunge bath measuring 25 by 40 feet. The well, just to the right in the photograph in the small structure, reached a depth of 1,400 feet and produced 1,500 barrels of artesian water that contained salt and sulfur. The artesian well began to run dry in 1876 and the hotel was destroyed by fire in either 1876 or 1879. There is some discrepancy over the date of the fire. (FPML/CADL.)

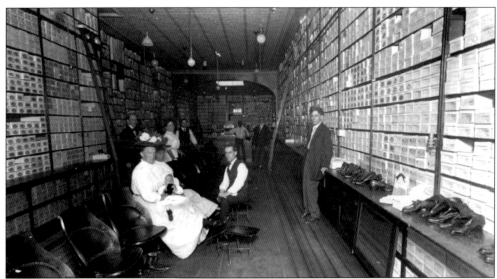

WOODWORTH SHOES, LOCATED AT 125 NORTH WASHINGTON AVENUE, C. 1898. Henry A. Woodworth opened this store in the 1860s, and it existed until Seymour Woodworth left to open a medical practice in Illinois in 1932. Henry A. Woodworth was still alive in 1932 but he retired and the business changed hands. It was briefly known as Reeds Shoes, but did not survive the Great Depression. (FPLH/CADL.)

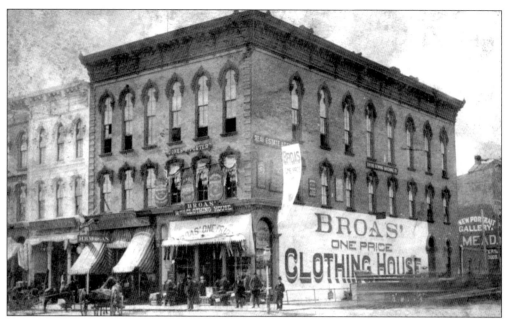

THE CLOTHING STORE WITH "OVER 5,000 VARIETIES IN SUITS FOR MEN AND BOYS TO SELECT FROM." Broas' One Price Clothing Store located at 101 East Michigan Avenue. Charles Broas had a variety of business interests in Lansing in the era before the First World War. Not only was he a clothing dealer, but he also was involved in real estate. The second floor housed the Davis Sewing Machine and the Tobacconist Roy Hardy Segar. Notice the sign for Mead Portrait Gallery in the background. (FPML/CADL.)

BROAS CLOTHING STORE HANDBILL, 1887. Banknote-sized advertising handbills with the look of currency were popular with businesses during the Victorian era. Broas One-Price Clothing House utilized this National Base Ball League Season of 1887 handbill to promote their goods of clothing, hats, caps, and furnishing goods. The face of the "note" features an image of the League's manager, W.H. Watkins, at the left and a uniformed Detroit batter at the right, while the back depicts portraits of the Detroit players.

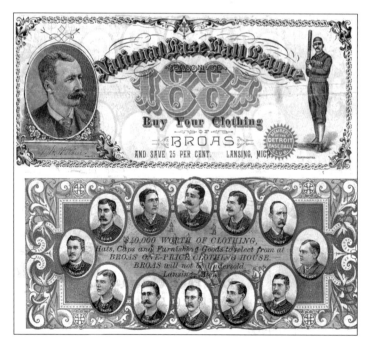

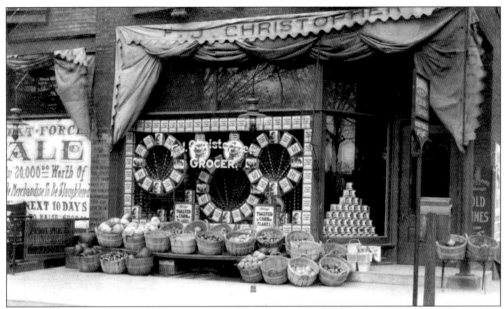

GROCER F.J. CHRISTOPHER OPERATED A STORE AT 1149 SOUTH WASHINGTON AVENUE.
The store at one time featured a wonderful Kellogg's Toasted Corn Flake display in the front
window. Christopher operated the store from 1905 until 1913. Frank J. Christopher had an
eventful life in Lansing. He served as a member of North Lansing Station Hose Company No.
2 in 1904 and was present at the Bryan Hotel fire, where he was almost killed by collapse of
the east wall. (FPML/CADL.)

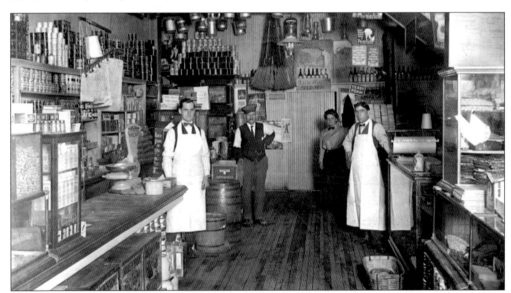

F.J. CHRISTOPHER'S GROCERY. Not only did F.J. Christopher stock fresh vegetables, he also
sold many well-known name brands such as Kar-A-Van Blend Coffee, Quaker Puffed Rice, and
Pearline Soap. Pearline Soap had an interesting sales slogan: "Avoid Mistakes count your
change before leaving buy Pearline Soap." After Frank Christopher left the grocery business he
became alderman for the 6th ward and later become city assessor in 1930. No one in the
photograph is identified. (FPML/CADL.)

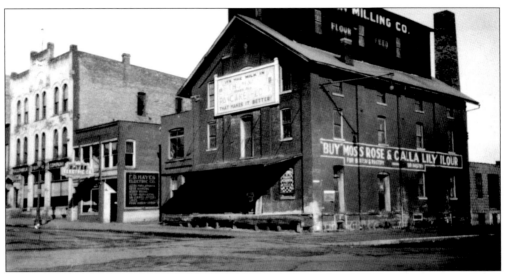

THE THOMAN MILL. This mill was built in 1857 and located at 125 East Ottawa near Grand Avenue. The Thoman name was first associated with the mill in 1868, when Frederick Thoman partnered with a gentleman named Rietz and purchased the mill. Later in 1868, Fredrick's brother became his partner and the Thoman family had sole ownership of the mill until its liquidation in 1957. In 1880 the mill had a capacity of 100 barrels of flour per 24 hours. A 75-horsepower steam engine provided the power for the mill's operation. The date on the photo is 1935. (FPML/CADL.)

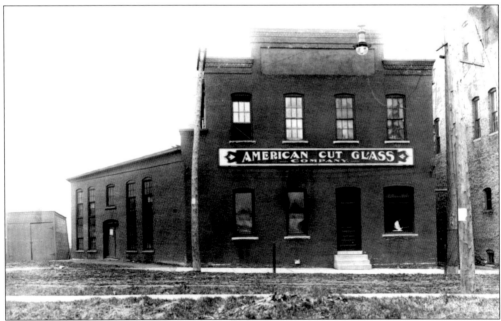

ONE OF LANSING'S GLASS FACTORIES. Although American Cut Glass was not originally a Lansing company, owner William C. Anderson relocated the company from Chicago around 1901. By 1914 Anderson had left Lansing and Patrick J. Healy managed the company. American Cut Glass was located at 710 East Kalamazoo until 1920 when the company went out of business. The American Cut Glass registered several interesting cut glass designs with the U.S. Patent Office, the best known were the "Radiant Star" and the "Pin Wheel." (FPML/CADL.)

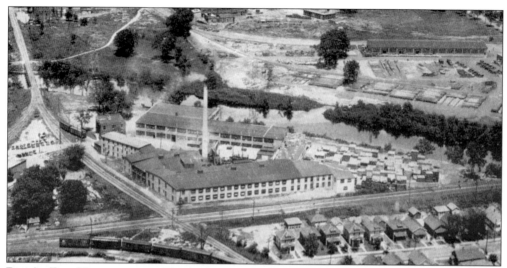

BIRD'S EYE VIEW OF THE HUGH LYONS & COMPANY FIXTURE FACTORY, C. 1920S.
Established in 1886, Hugh Lyons & Company originally manufactured a product called "The Hat Conformator" in a building on Washington Avenue. The company later manufactured store window display fixtures as well as auto truck bodies at 700 East South Street. Hugh Lyons served as Lansing's mayor during 1904–1907.

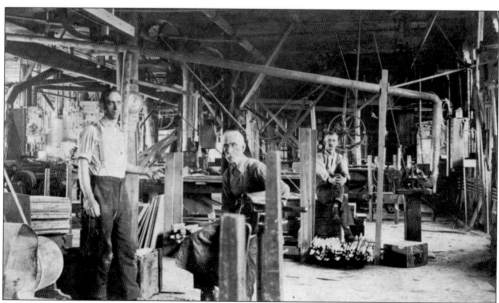

WOODSHOP, HUGH LYONS & COMPANY. This is an interior view of the factory woodshop with carpenters Charles Pulcifer, Fred Pulcifer, and Ed Hoffman.

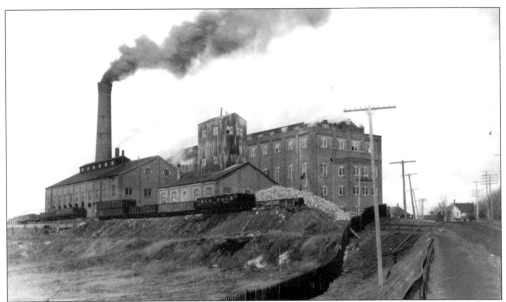

THE LANSING SUGAR PLANT. The plant has been known by several names throughout its history: the Owosso Sugar Plant, the Lansing Sugar Plant, and finally in 1924, the Michigan Sugar Plant. Located on what is today known as North Grand River, the plant was just to the left after crossing the bridge over the Grand River as one was heading north. It was built in 1901 by the Cleveland firm Kilby Manufacturing Company, which also supplied the machinery. The plant was torn down in 1954. (FPML/CADL.)

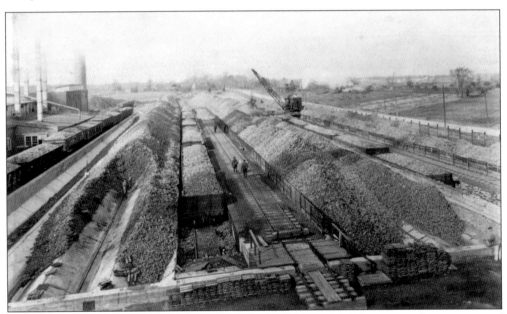

UNLOADING SUGAR BEETS. The Lansing Sugar Plant processed a tremendous amount of sugar beets. Each freight car carried 52 tons of sugar beets, and on an average day over 500 tons would arrive. The plant ran three shifts and employed over 250 men. In 1902 the plant produced 500 barrels of sugar a day. In 1934 alone, the plant produced 35,000 tons of sugar. Just to the right in the photograph is U.S. 16.

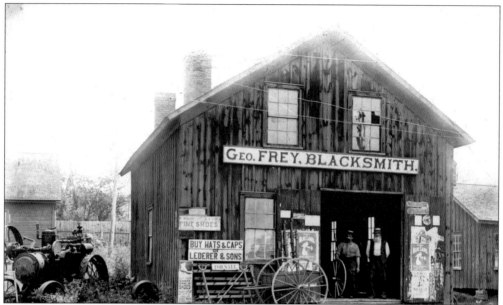

THE GEORGE FREY BLACKSMITH SHOP AT 1240 TURNER IN NORTH LANSING. George Frey began his blacksmith shop in 1904 at 736 Turner Street in North Lansing. Either he moved his shop or the address changed during the frequent renumbering of streets that occurred at this time. In 1928 he was still operating his blacksmith shop on Turner. Notice the tractor next to the building and that the shop is selling hats, caps, and shoes. (FPML/CADL.)

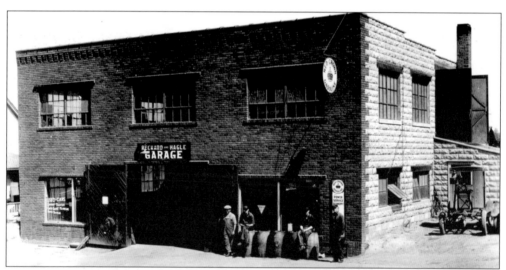

THE RECKARD AND HAGLE GARAGE. Located at 1411 East Kalamazoo and owned by Adelbert E. "Dell" Reckard and his half-brother Henry H. "Jack" Hagle. Built in 1924, the garage serviced the needs of the growing motoring public. The garage sold Red Crown Gasoline and the pumps were located just out of the photograph to the right. The Reckards and Hagle had the capability to pull cars onto the second floor using the ramp that is visible in the right-hand corner of this image. The brothers sold used cars, and the ad in the window tells us that at this time in 1926, they offered a Dodge Touring automobile, a Cole-Eight Touring automobile, and a Ford Touring automobile, all like new. (FPML/CADL.)

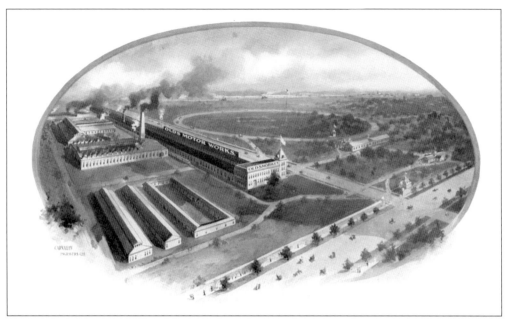

BIRD'S EYE VIEW OF THE OLDS MOTOR WORKS, 1902. A second Lansing factory of the Olds Motor Works was built on the former site of the Michigan State Fair Grounds. Established in 1880, P.F. Olds & Son manufactured steam engines, brass and iron castings, and steam yachts. In 1883, Ransom E. Olds joined his father's company as a bookkeeper and machinist. In 1890 the company was incorporated as Olds Gasoline Engine Works and in 1899 this firm and the Olds Motor Vehicle Company were merged and reincorporated as the Olds Motor Works.

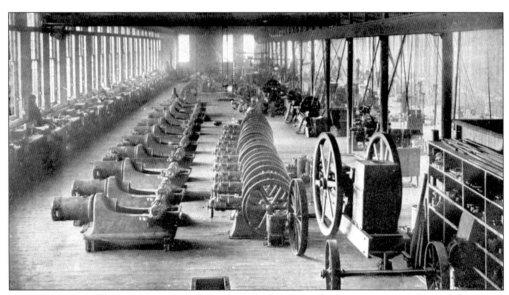

OLDS GASOLINE ENGINE ERECTING FLOOR, 1902. Thousands of stationary gasoline engines were produced by the company providing between one and 50 horsepower and priced between $200 and $2,400. Later the company would expand its line and offer huge stationary engines up to 300 horsepower. The engines were used to pump water from the ground, saw raw lumber into boards, split firewood, mill, and generate the power needed for the large manufacturing plants.

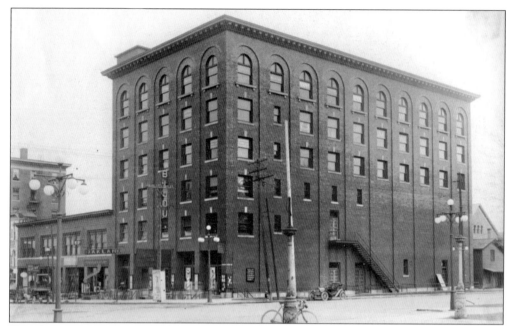

THE OAKLAND BUILDING. Located at the corner of Capitol and Michigan Avenues, was one of Lansing's oldest and largest structures until it was destroyed by fire in 1923. The Oakland Building housed several of the smaller state agencies, i.e. the Michigan Railway Commission, the State Board of Registration of Nursing, and the State Game Fish and Forestry Warden. The Oakland building was also home to the Regent/Bijou Theater. The Romney Building, formerly the Olds Hotel, now stands on this site. (FPLH/CADL.)

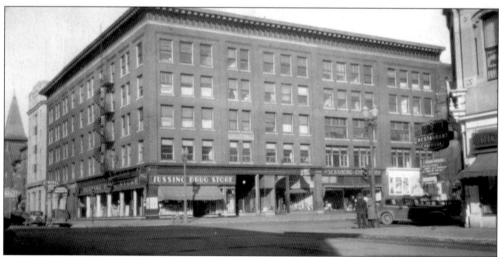

A STREET VIEW OF NORTH WASHINGTON AND OTTAWA STREET IN 1935 WITH THE TUSSING BUILDING DOMINATING THE CORNER. The Tussing Building, constructed in 1909 and 1910, was designed by Darius Moon and was five stories tall. It had 132 feet of frontage on Washington and 153 feet of frontage on Ottawa. In fact, the building was considered to sit on Ottawa Street and not Washington. The Plaza Theater was located in the Tussing Building, and at the time this photograph was taken, it was showing the movie *Thirty Day Princess* starring Sylvia Sidney and Cary Grant. (FPML/CADL.)

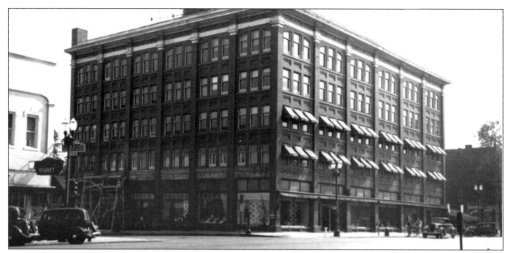

ARBAUGH'S DEPARTMENT STORE, LOCATED AT 401 SOUTH WASHINGTON AVENUE. Constructed in 1904 and 1905, this structure was the first skyscraper in Lansing. Frank Arbaugh, along with partner B.C. Cameron, agreed to construct a large department store to be known as Cameron & Arbaugh. In 1909, Arbaugh bought out his partner and the business became known as F.N. Arbaugh Company. Frank Arbaugh was an innovator in the retail industry; he opened a self-serve grocery in the basement and provided free parking to his patrons. In 1953 the interest in the Arbaugh Department store was sold to the Sperry and Hutchinson Company, which operated the Wurzburg Department Stores. In 1969 the store was renamed Wurzburg's, but closed in 1973. Frank Arbaugh died in March 1955. (FPML/CADL.)

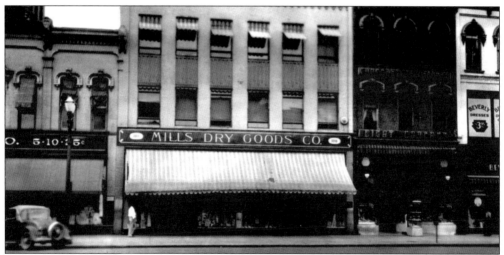

THE MILLS DRY GOODS STORE WAS THE EPITOME OF THE AMERICAN DREAM. Originally a small dry goods store in Mason, Michigan, the business moved to Lansing in 1905. It grew so quickly that in 1910, Mills Dry Goods acquired Lansing Dry Goods and moved to 108–110 South Washington Avenue. The photograph shows the dry goods store soon after a major renovation in 1931 when the iron portico that graced the entrance to the store was removed. In 1941 the firm would move across the street to 113 South Washington where it operated until its closing in 1960. Fredrick E. Mills managed the business in Lansing until his death in 1946. His son, Lucius Mills, supervised the store until it was sold to the F.W. Uhlman Company in 1959, resulting in the closing of the business in December of 1960. (FPML/CADL.)

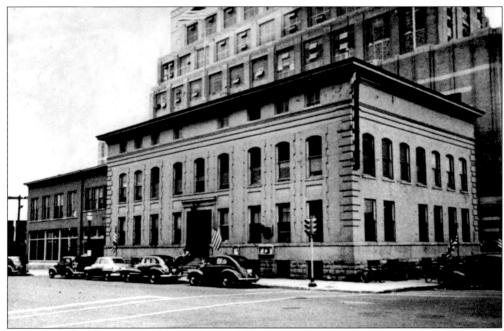

THE OFFICE OF THE *STATE JOURNAL*, 1915–1950. Located at 200–210 North Grand just north of the Hotel Kerns, this structure was built in 1903 and remodeled in 1930 for the then-enormous sum of $250,000. The remodeling included not only alterations to both buildings, but the purchase of new presses and office equipment. Lawrence & Van Buren Printing Company originally occupied 210 North Grand. The Board of Water and Light tore down the building in 1954. The site was originally home to Bement and Sons. (FPML/CADL.)

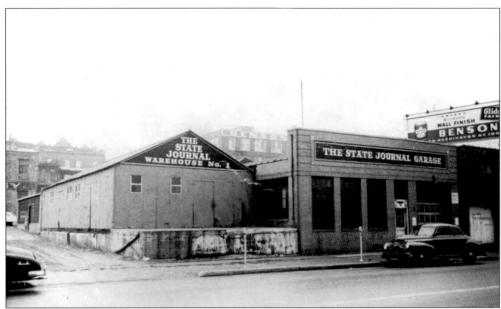

THE STATE JOURNAL GARAGE AND PAPER STORAGE FACILITY WAS LOCATED AT 219–221 NORTH GRAND. Almost directly across from the main *State Journal* building, the garage had the capacity to house 30 vehicles and was built in the 1930s at a cost of $19,000. (FPML/CADL.)

Three

AUTOMOBILE CAPITAL

RANSOM ELI OLDS, 1864–1950.
Lansing auto pioneer, Ransom Eli Olds,
developed and manufactured the first
popular automobile, the Curved Dash
Runabout, and the assembly line. R.E.
Olds was born in Geneva, Ohio in 1864
and moved to Lansing with his parents
in 1880. During 1886, R.E. Olds
developed a vehicle powered by a
stationary steam engine. In 1896 Olds
assembled a vehicle with a gas engine
and a body built by the Clark Carriage
Co. The inventor, along with several
local investors, formed the Olds Motor
Vehicle Co. in 1897 which evolved into
the Olds Motor Works. Olds left the
company in 1904 and established the
REO Motor Car Co. and remained at
the head of the company through 1936.

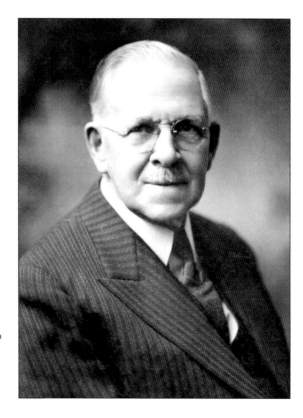

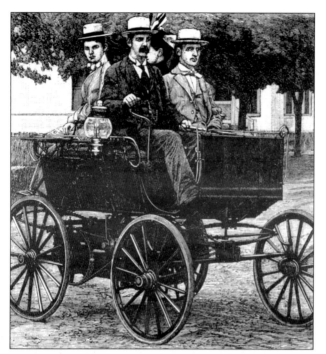

OLDS' INTERNAL-COMBUSTION ENGINE VEHICLE, 1896. The Olds horseless carriage, as depicted in this contemporary wood-cut illustration, shows Ransom E. Olds at the tiller with carriage builder Frank G. Clark as his front seat passenger. Seated at the rear are Mrs. Clark, left, and Mrs. Olds. A five-horsepower gasoline motor provided the vehicle with a maximum speed of 18 miles per hour.

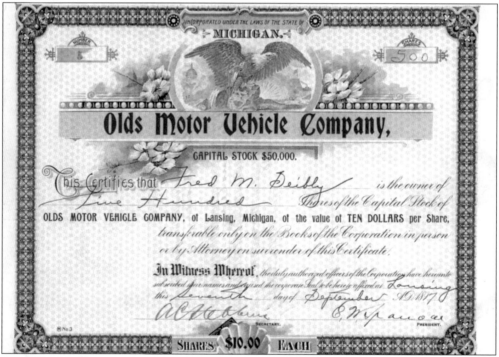

OLDS MOTOR VEHICLE COMPANY STOCK CERTIFICATE, 1897. On August 21, 1897, the first company organized in Michigan to manufacture an automobile was formed. The officers of the company included E.W. Sparrow, president, Arthur C. Stebbins, secretary, and Ransom E. Olds as manager. A resolution passed at the directors' meeting authorized Mr. Olds "... to build one carriage in as nearly perfect a manner as possible. . . ."

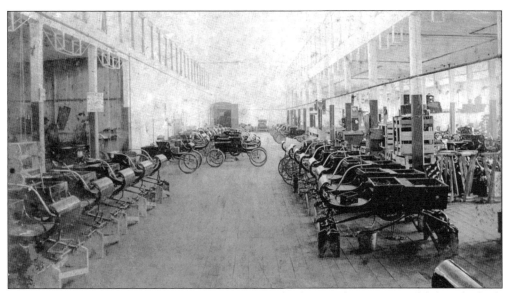

OLDS MOTOR WORKS ASSEMBLY LINE, c. 1902. The first production automobile to be built in quantity was the famous Curved Dash Runabout. This photograph features rows of the popular Oldsmobile in various stages of completion in the Lansing plant. Olds Motor Works employed 416 employees during 1902 and produced 2,500 automobiles. The engine plant employed an additional 160.

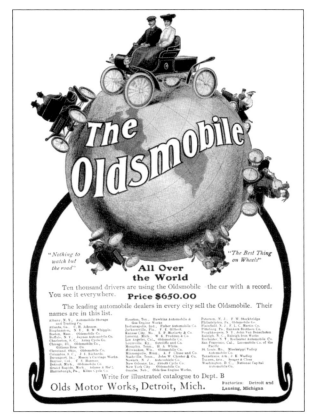

THE OLDSMOBILE, 1903. "Nothing to watch but the road" and "The Best Thing on Wheels" were the early advertising slogans of the Olds Motor Works. In 1902, Roy D. Chapin completed a nine-day cross-country run in the Curved Dash Oldsmobile from Detroit to New York for advertising purposes.

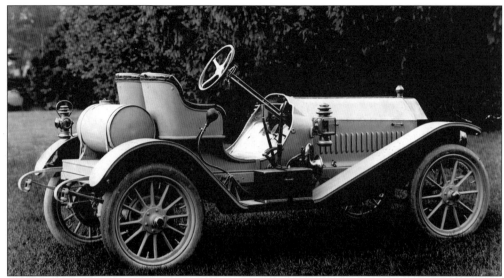

THE STRIKING 1910 OLDSMOBILE SPECIAL ROADSTER. The two-door roadster had a four-cylinder engine, a four-speed transmission, and cost $3,000. It carried an external gas tank mounted on the trunk. Total production for the 1910 Special series, which included the four-door touring and the four-door limo, was 1,000 units. The 1910 Oldsmobile Special Roadster was a powerful automobile with an eye-catching appearance. (Caterino/CADL.)

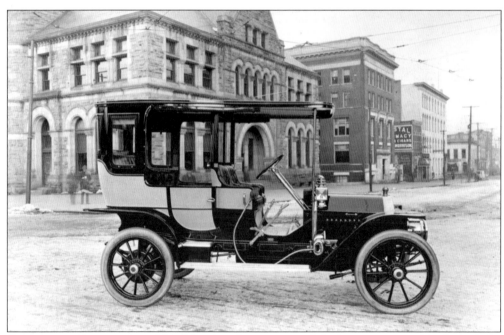

OLDSMOBILE LIMOUSINE, 1908. This handsome automobile features a caned body built by Oldsmobile on the M series chassis. The 1908 Oldsmobile catalog noted "For winter use or special functions, limousines are rapidly gaining favor among the exclusive set and no expense has been spared to make them acceptable to the most fastidious." Weather protection was provided by roll-up side curtains. The Lansing Post Office, located on the southwest corner of Capitol and Michigan, is in the background.

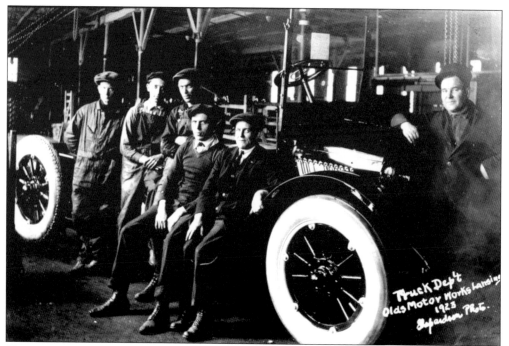

THE MEN OF THE TRUCK DEPARTMENT OLDS MOTOR WORKS, 1923. From right to left in the photograph are William Heuschele, J.R. Chase, Vern Yallup, F. Chase, and the last two are unknown. (FPML/CADL.)

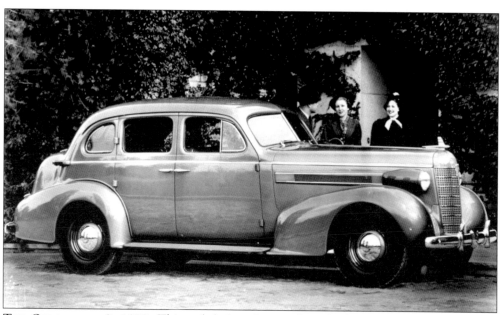

THE OLDSMOBILE 8, 1937. This stylish four-door, eight-cylinder touring sedan with trunk was promoted as "The car that has Everything." Oldsmobile production for 1937 totaled 206,086 vehicles including three different Coupes, two- and four-door Sedans, and Touring Sedans. During 1937 Oldsmobile introduced the Safety Automatic Transmission, a transmission that shifted by itself.

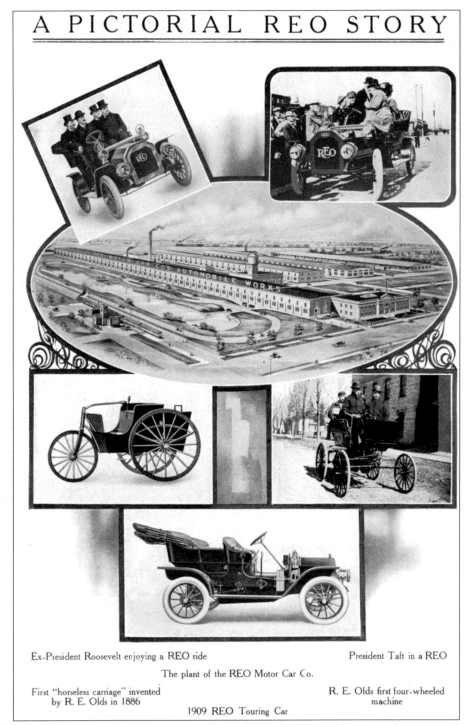

Ex-President Roosevelt enjoying a REO ride

President Taft in a REO

The plant of the REO Motor Car Co.

First "horseless carriage" invented
by R. E. Olds in 1886

R. E. Olds first four-wheeled
machine

1909 REO Touring Car

REO MOTOR CAR COMPANY, c. 1909. This ad features historic milestones and moments in the career of R.E. Olds. In 1909, three reliable REOs were available including a Five-Passenger Touring Car priced at $1,000; a Two or Four-Passenger Roadster at $1,000, or the Two-Passenger Runabout at $500. Founded in 1904, The REO Motor Car Company produced automobiles through 1936.

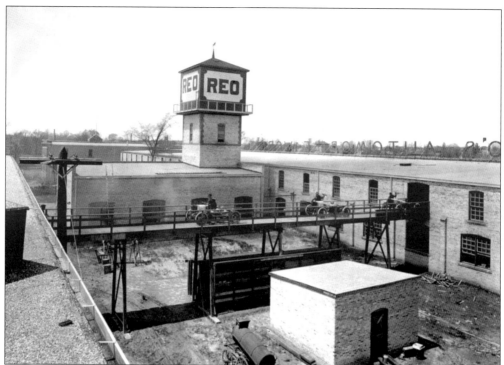

REO MOTOR CAR COMPANY, 1905. This rare photograph depicts the bridge between the manufacturing buildings with employees walking the automobile chassis across to the next stage in production. The weathervane on top of the tower featured an REO automobile. Automobile production during 1905 totaled 864 and reached its peak in 1927 with 33,353 vehicles. In its final year of production, 1936, the company manufactured 3,206 automobiles.

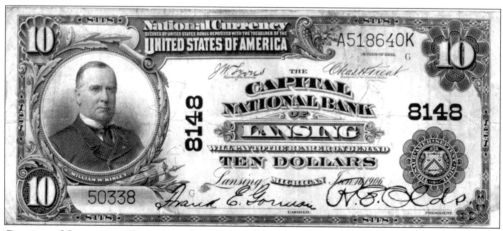

CAPITAL NATIONAL BANK OF LANSING, $10 LARGE SIZE BANKNOTE. The Capital National Bank was organized by automotive pioneer Ransom E. Olds, whose printed signature appears as the bank President. In the denominations of $10 and $20, $6,440,920 worth of banknotes were issued between 1906 and 1934. The bank failed during the depression and was placed into receivership on March 13, 1934. For a number of years the bank was located in the Hollister building on the northwest corner of Allegan and Washington Avenues until the Olds Tower was completed in 1931.

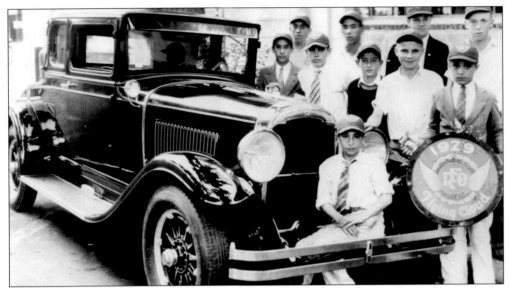

REO FLYING CLOUD STANDARD COUPE, 1929. The REO Flying Cloud was promoted as "the Master" with the 1929 sales catalog featuring ten models for the buyer to consider. The Standard Coupe was described as "The young business man, the professional man, the woman who shops and can't wait for her packages to be delivered—these are candidates for a car that keeps the snappy roadster feeling even in a closed model. Speed— smartness— and comfort against all weather—are combined." Members of an unidentified REO boys' baseball team gather to promote the model.

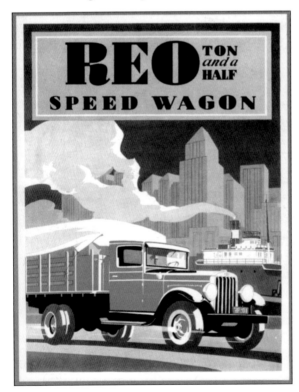

REO SPEEDWAGON SALES BROCHURE, 1931. REO was not only known for its automobiles but also for its truck production. This wonderful art deco cover features a "ton and a half" platform stake body truck powered with the famous 6-cylinder Gold Crown engine cast of chrome nickel alloy.

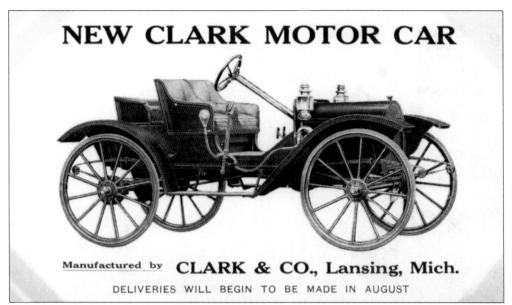

NEW CLARK MOTOR CAR

Manufactured by **CLARK & CO., Lansing, Mich.**

DELIVERIES WILL BEGIN TO BE MADE IN AUGUST

CLARK MOTOR CAR, ADVERTISING CARD, c. 1910–1911. Another Lansing automotive pioneer was Frank G. Clark, who manufactured carriages with his father Albert from the late 1860s. In 1902 he organized the Clarkmobile Company, and introduced his first automobile in 1903. In 1905 he sold his business to the New Way Motor Co. In 1910, Frank Clark organized Clark & Co. for the purpose of producing a two-cylinder, 14-horsepower vehicle. Once again, his automotive concern was short-lived and he turned his efforts to manufacturing trucks in Pontiac, where he founded the Columbia Motor Truck Co.

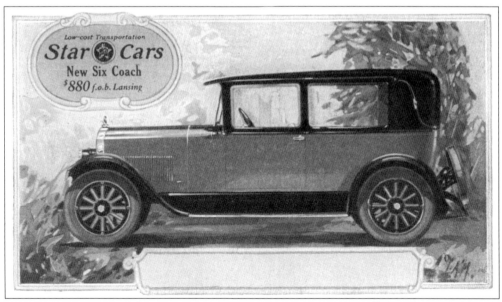

Low-cost Transportation
Star Cars
New Six Coach
$880 f.o.b. Lansing

DURANT MOTORS STAR SIX COACH, ADVERTISING CARD, c. 1926. Following his second forced departure from General Motors, William C. Durant re-entered the automobile industry with his own car company and began the production of the Durant and the Star in 1922. The Durant Motor Car Co. plant was located on Verlinden. Durant Motors ceased production in 1930.

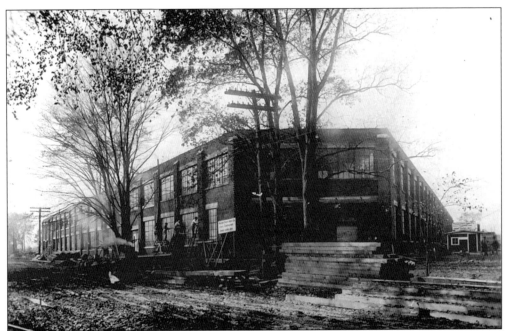

THE DUPLEX TRUCK COMPANY PLANT UNDER CONSTRUCTION IN NOVEMBER 1917. The plant was located on the corner of South Washington and Mt. Hope; it opened on December 1, 1917, employing 300 workers. Duplex Truck was eventually sold to Warner & Swasey of Cleveland in 1955. (FPML/CADL.)

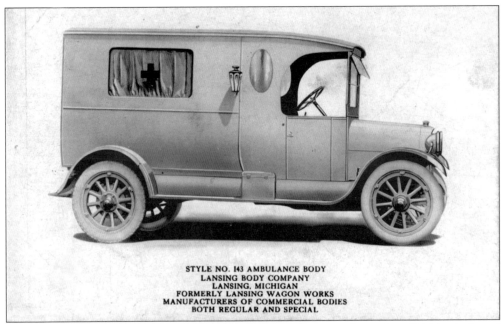

STYLE NO. 143 AMBULANCE BODY
LANSING BODY COMPANY
LANSING, MICHIGAN
FORMERLY LANSING WAGON WORKS
MANUFACTURERS OF COMMERCIAL BODIES
BOTH REGULAR AND SPECIAL

AMBULANCE BODY, c. 1920s. The Lansing Body Company, was located at 504 North Grand Avenue. Company officers included O.F. Barnes, president, E.F. Cooley, vice-president, F.H. Thoman, secretary-treasurer, and Bruce E. Anderson, general manager.

Four
PUBLIC SERVICE

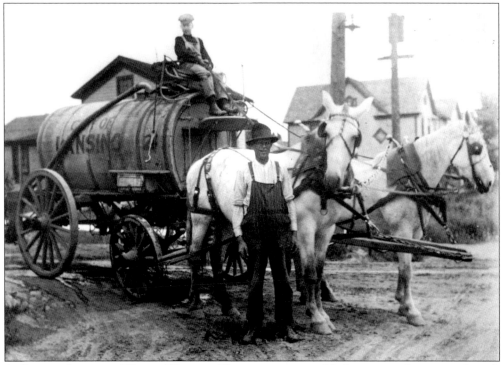

A CITY OF LANSING WATER WAGON. These wagons sprinkled water on the unpaved roads in an effort to keep down the dust. In an era of unpaved roads, these wagons were appreciated in the summer months when the blowing dirt would have penetrated every home and business. (FPML/CADL.)

Remonstrance.

To the Common Council of the City of Lansing, the undersigned respectfully ask your honorable body not to repeal the ordinance of 1874, which excludes Cattle from the Streets and Sidewalks of the City, as we believe the people have Superior rights on said Streets & Sidewalks to any Animals, and that the benefit claimed for a few, should yield to the interests and Safety of the many.

C. Cortice   C. Christopher
C. Tracy   C A Damson
John S Jennings   C E Kauflawnut
J Van Orner   D D White
S. Edson   G Warren
Johan Speitel   Mrs Ida Cline
A Cline
Frank Chaffee   Mrs D C Hurd
J VanHusen   Geo W B

A WONDERFUL EXAMPLE OF DEMOCRACY IN ACTION IN EARLY LANSING. The petition was asking the Lansing City Council not to repeal the 1874 city ordinance that prohibited cows from wandering the streets of Lansing. The council repealed the ordinance, and for a short time, cattle were allowed to roam freely throughout the city, grazing. After a massive outcry by the citizens of Lansing, the ordinance was quickly reinstated and cattle were no longer allowed to graze among the streets, making the city safer as well as much cleaner. (FPML/CADL.)

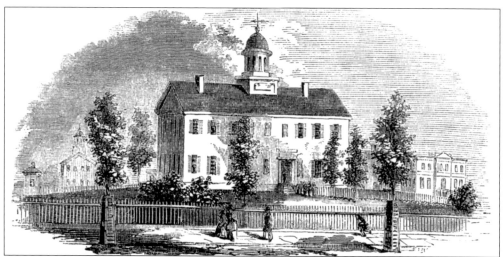

FIRST CAPITOL BUILDING IN LANSING, 1847–1879. This c. 1850s woodcut features the first Capitol at Lansing, from the east, as it would have appeared between 1847 and 1865, when an addition of 16 feet was made to the south end. Ten of the state's governors served within the building, which also accommodated the house and senate chambers. The building on the right, located on the site of the present capitol, contained the office of Secretary of State and Auditor, among others. The building was completely destroyed by fire on December 16, 1882.

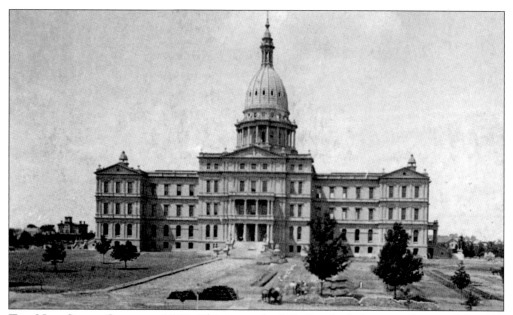

THE NEW STATE CAPITOL, 1879. This image, by J.H. Scotford, shows work around the new capitol nearing completion. Construction of the capitol was well underway when the ceremony for the laying of the cornerstone took place on October 2, 1873. More than 30,000 attended the event. The capitol was formally dedicated and Governor Charles Croswell was inaugurated for a second term on January 1, 1879. This beautiful finished masterpiece was designed by the architect Elijah E. Myers. The building measures over 420 feet long, 273 feet wide, and 267 feet high. Restoration of the historic landmark was undertaken in 1988 and completed in 1992, recapturing its early Victorian splendor.

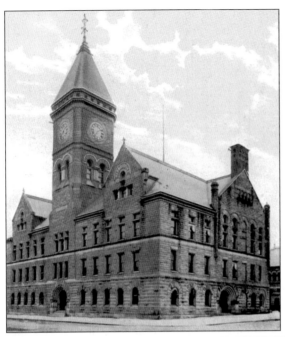

CITY HALL, 1896–1958. Lansing City Hall, the first municipally-owned building, opened in 1896 on the northeast corner of Ottawa and Capitol Avenues. During the same year, the Police Department relocated their headquarters to the back of the new building and the city hall clock tower began striking on "standard time," instead of "sun" or local time, which varied 20 to 25 minutes from standard time. Construction on the present city hall building started on February 1, 1955, at a cost of $4.5 million, and the building opened in May of 1958. In 1959 the old city hall building was razed.

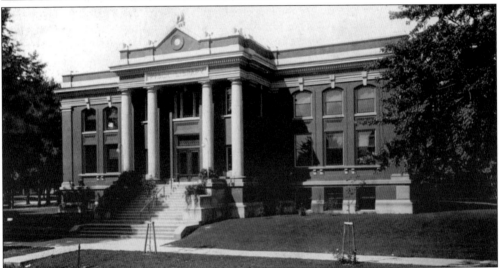

LANSING'S CARNEGIE LIBRARY IN THE EARLY 1900S. Lansing's original public library was located in the high school building for 22 years. In 1897 the library was moved to the old city hall building, and thanks to the aid of the Ladies Library Association and the Young Men's Society, the library's collection grew to 13,000 volumes. Later, the State Librarian Mrs. Mary C. Spencer corresponded with Andrew Carnegie and obtained the promise of $35,000 for a new building provided the city would furnish a site and provide $3,500 a year to maintain the library. The building, located at 310 West Shiawassee, was constructed of red pressed brick with accents of Amherst stone and had the capacity to house 20,000 volumes. The library opened in 1905 and served the needs of the community until 1964 when a new library was opened on South Capitol Avenue. Currently the building is owned by Lansing Community College and serves as an educational facility. The building is an outstanding example of the architectural style of that period. (FPML/CADL.)

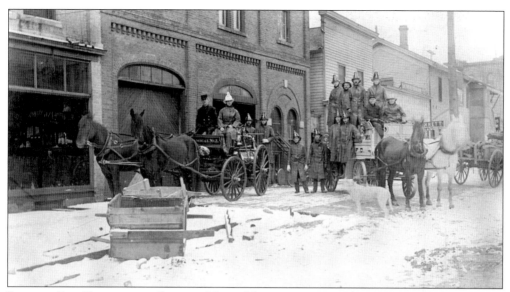

LANSING FIRE DEPARTMENT STATION NO. 1, MARCH 27, 1904. The organization of the Lansing Fire Department (LFD) is recorded in the Proceedings of Torrent Engine Co. No. 1 for October 5, 1857, where, "A meeting of the Citizens of Lansing was held (*for*) the organization of a fire department for the better protection of the property of the citizens of Lansing for the purpose of perfecting such organization." On October 27, 1857, a constitution and by-laws were adopted. Prior to its organization, the only protection against fire was a volunteer ladder and bucket brigade.

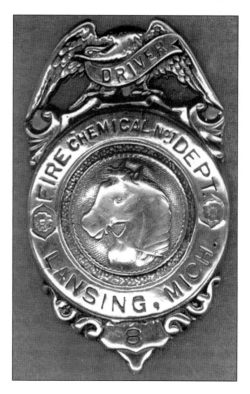

LFD CHEMICAL NO. 1 DRIVER'S BADGE, c. 1890–1910. Horse-drawn chemical apparatus was typically the first line of defense for the community until the steamer was ready for pumping water. In the 1904 photograph of LFD Station No. 1 featured above, Chemical Co. No. 1 is on the left, and Hose Co. No. 1 is on the right. This firemen's badge recalls the glory days of the horse-drawn apparatus by featuring a horse head as its central design. During this period, George B. Andrews was the driver of Chemical No. 1.

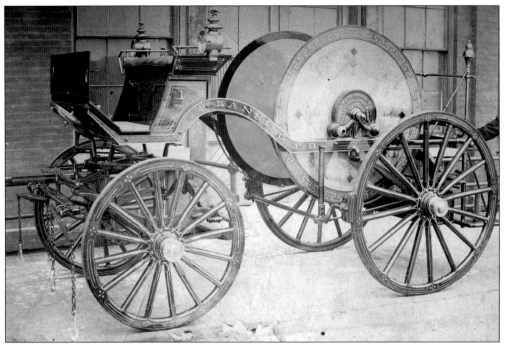

LANSING FIRE DEPARTMENT HORSE-DRAWN HOSE CARRIAGE NO. 1, c. 1880s. This beautiful and important piece of a fire department apparatus was built by E.B. Preston & Co., fire department apparatus manufacturers of Chicago. This rare photograph was probably taken during the arrival of the hose carriage before being placed in service with a full reel of leather hose. The reel allowed for the quick release of the hose and made retrieval much easier. Soon hose wagons would replace the reel.

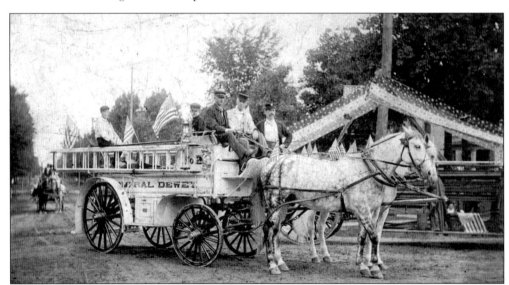

LFD HOOK AND LADDER CO. NO. 2, c. 1900. This hook and ladder truck was named the "Admiral Dewey," in honor of the hero of Manila Bay following the Spanish-American War in 1898. This photograph depicts the horse-drawn apparatus ready for a parade adorned by many American flags.

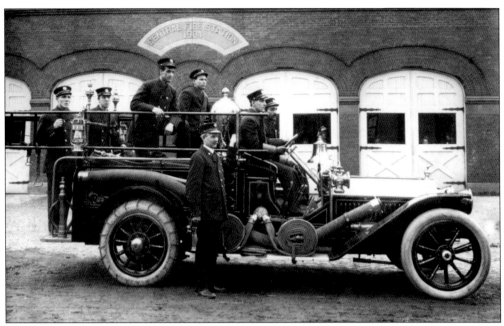

LFD Auto Fire Engine, 1908. The era of horse-drawn fire apparatus would soon fade into history when Fire Chief Hugo R. Delfs, standing in front, ordered the first automobile fire engine built in the United States for the Lansing department. The chassis was built by the Olds Motor Works and shipped to The Webb Pump Company, St. Louis, Missouri, which installed a rotary type pump. The engine was thoroughly tested before being placed into service on December 16, 1908. The total cost was $6,500.

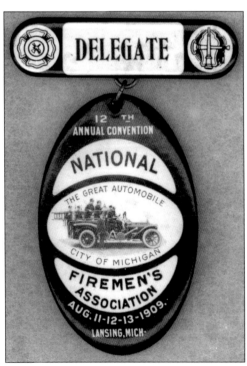

National Firemen's Association 12th Annual Convention Badge, 1909. Members of the National Fireman's Association gathered in Lansing, August 11–13, 1909, for their annual convention and were able to view first hand the star attraction—the first automobile fire engine in the United States. This rare convention badge features the image shown right along with the slogan, "The Great Automobile City of Michigan." The automobile industry took the leading role in the evolution of fire department apparatus, putting an end to horse-drawn fire equipment by the early 1920s .

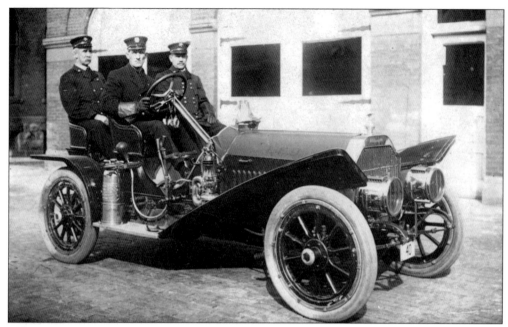

LFD Chief's Car, c. 1910. The chief's automobile was this classy 1907–1908 Oldsmobile Flying Roadster seen here in front of Central Station No. 1 at the base of Allegan Street on Grand Avenue. Chief Hugo R. Delfs is seated in the back; also pictured is Frank B. Edison, driver, and to his left is Assistant Chief George B. Andrews.

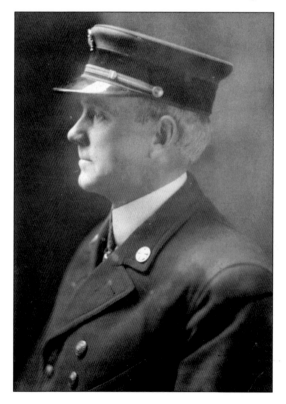

Fire Chief Hugo R. Delfs. Chief Delfs's leadership revolutionized the Lansing Fire Department during the early part of the 20th century. Appointed on February 1, 1904, he held the office continuously until his death in 1941. There were only two stations when he joined the department in 1890. Teams were maintained for a chemical wagon, two hose carts, and a hook and ladder wagon. In 1940, the department grew to 8 stations, staffed by 112 full time firefighters, and 16 pieces of motorized equipment.

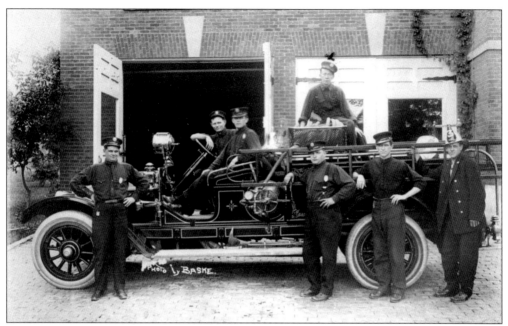

LFD FIRE STATION NO. 3, 1914. This 1914 photograph features the engine company with one of their first auto fire engines. Standing are Forest C. Perry, Med J. Dumeney, Earl M. Pettit, and Charles H. Tomrell; seated are unidentified, Harry G. Beghold, driver, and Claude Harrington. Station No. 3 was located at 630 West Hillsdale Street.

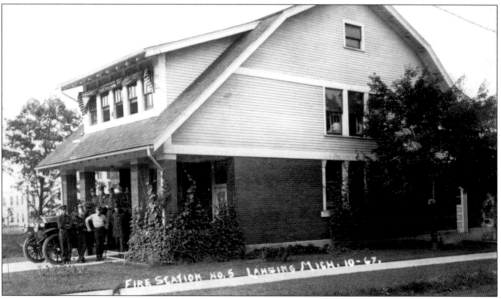

LFD STATION NO. 5, 1916. In the 1910 Annual Report of the Lansing Board of Police and Fire Commissioners, Chief Hugo Delfs recommended that a station be built in the south part of the city. He went on to recommend that the station be equipped with a combination chemical and hose wagon and that five firemen be placed to properly man the apparatus. Within a few years Station No. 5 was built at 1439 South Washington Avenue, just south of the REO Motor Car Company factory.

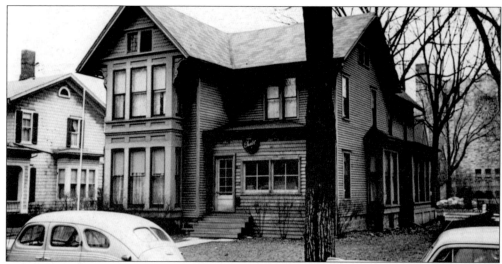

LANSING'S SECOND HOSPITAL, LOCATED AT 310 WEST OTTAWA. In 1896, 100 local women met at the Downey Hotel to form the Woman's Hospital Association. The organization took over the "DeViney Place" on Ottawa Street, and Dr. Rush Shank performed an operation, an amputation, on the hospital's first patient. The patient survived and two and a half years later the hospital moved to the Moffatt House on South Grand. It later moved to the Mead home on South Cedar, where it remained until the opening of Sparrow Hospital in 1912. The site at 310 West Ottawa is now a parking lot. (FPML/CADL.)

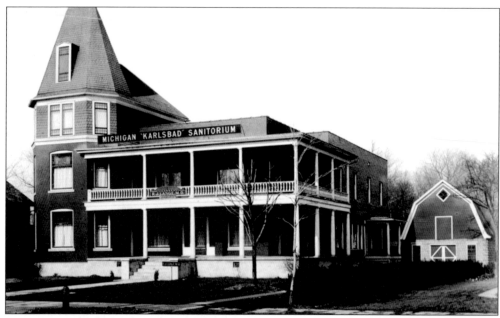

THE MICHIGAN KARLSBAD SANITORIUM LOCATED AT 101 EAST WILLOW. It offered the finest baths and masseurs for the treatment of gout, lumbago, constipation, and a list of other complaints. The sanitorium offered private bathing and rest rooms as well as a dock so that patients could arrive by boat. The facility was managed by Dr. Rudolph J. Lange and operated until 1920 when St. Lawrence Hospital acquired the site. The building is still standing, though the structure has been slightly modified. (Caterino/CADL.)

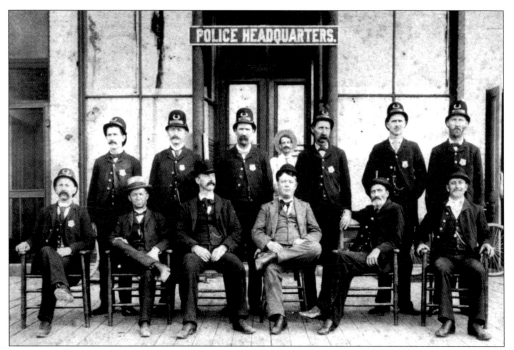

LANSING POLICE DEPARTMENT, C. 1894. The Lansing Police Department was officially formed in 1893. John P. Sanford (front row, center) was appointed first Chief of Police effective August 3, 1893. The 1893 budget administered by Chief Sanford included salaries of $7,380. Other costs included the feeding of prisoners, $500; rent for jail, $500; clubs and belts, $23; as well as other expenses. (LPD Historical File.)

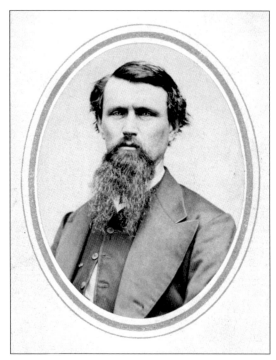

LEE C. HUTCHINSON, LANSING CITY MARSHAL, 1871–1872. The first law enforcement officials in Lansing were known as city marshals. Lansing became an incorporated city in 1859. Hiram Smith, Lansing's first mayor, appointed James P. Baker as the first city marshal. Published in 1878, *Mudge's Directory of Lansing City*, lists Hutchinson as "constable and deputy sheriff, 141 Wash'n Ave."

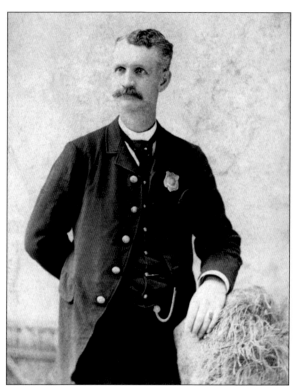

S. Benjamin Harrington, 1890. Prior to the official organization of the Lansing Police Department in 1893, the police department consisted of a marshal, patrolmen, and a turnkey. The Police Headquarters and City Jail were located at 204 East Michigan Avenue. Little is known about Officer Harrington, seen here in his single-breasted frock coat and wearing the first known badge style of the department. This cabinet photograph is signed and dated "Feby 23d 90" in Harrington's hand. His name appears in the 1891 city directory as residing at 164 North Larch. (Pat Heyden Collection.)

George E. Palmer, Truant Officer, 1904–1907. In 1906, Officer Palmer organized the Palmer Shoe Fund to provide shoes to needy students. George Palmer's legacy continues as The Old Newsboy Fund. (LPD Historical File.)

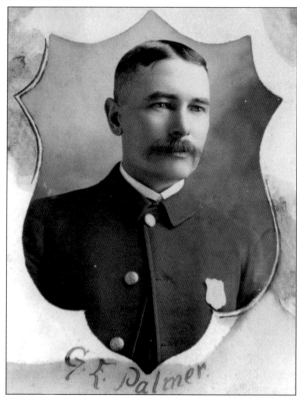

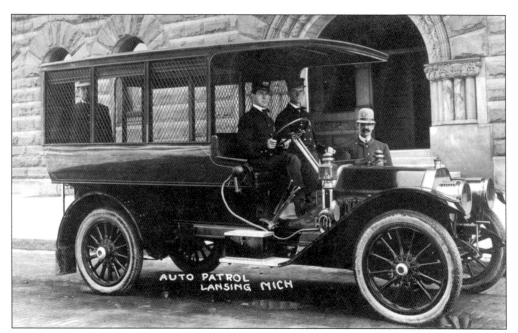

LANSING POLICE DEPARTMENT AUTO PATROL WAGON, C. 1909. During 1909 the Lansing Police Department, headed by Chief Behrendt, received on loan an Olds Touring car known as "The Black Maria." Light gauge wire was stretched across the back open areas to deter escapes. The Lansing Police Department was among the first in the nation to have an auto patrol.

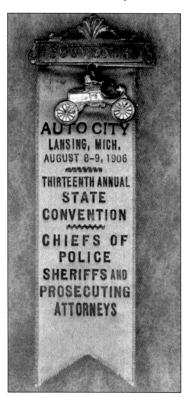

CHIEFS OF POLICE, SHERIFFS AND PROSECUTING ATTORNEYS 13TH ANNUAL STATE CONVENTION BADGE, 1906. Law enforcement officials from across the state gathered in Lansing, August 6–9, 1906, for their annual convention. This souvenir badge features a detailed brass charm of the popular Curved Dash Oldsmobile, manufactured in Lansing, the "AUTO CITY."

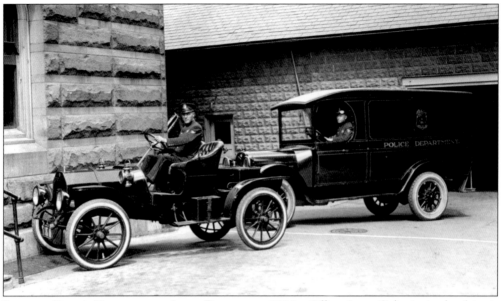

LANSING POLICE DEPARTMENT AUTO PATROL, C. 1920S. Officer Leon Cole sits in the driver's seat of the patrol car and Officer Leo Bauer in the patrol wagon. (Pat Heyden Collection.)

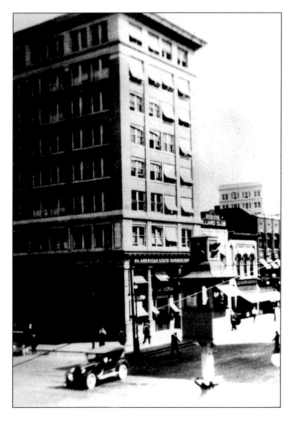

FIRST ELECTRIC LIGHT SIGNAL, C. 1922. The "Crow's Nest" replaced the manual stop and go sign at Michigan and Washington Avenues. A police officer sat in the tower and regulated traffic by ringing a bell to warn drivers the light would be changing. In 1926 the tower was replaced with an automatic overhead traffic signal. (LPD Historical File.)

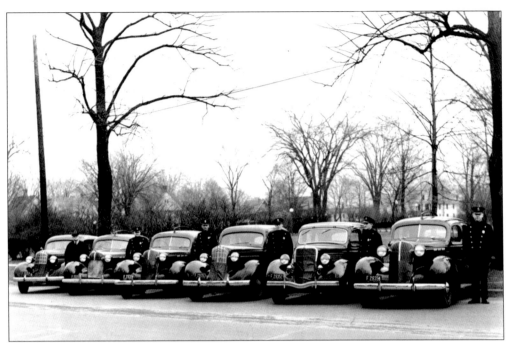

LPD Patrol Cars and Officers, 1937. In 1938, the Lansing Police Department modernized their patrol vehicles with the purchase of five two-way radio units, introducing an innovative tool of communication for law enforcement officers. (LPD Historical File.)

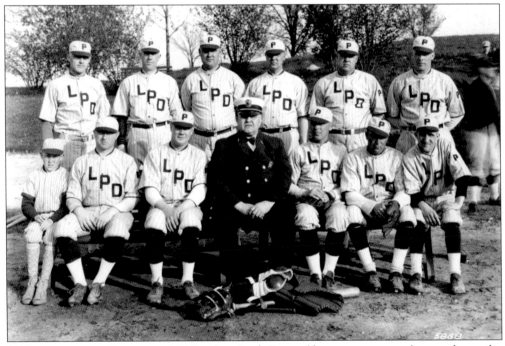

LPD Baseball Team, c. 1930s. Lt. Fred Fouts (front row, center) served on the department between 1910 and 1934. The rest of the players and the bat boy at the left are unidentified. (LPD Historical File.)

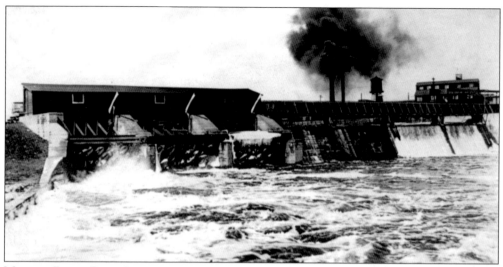

MOORES RIVER DAM. In 1898, Lansing City Council authorized the Piatt brothers to build a power generating plant near Moores Park. Later that year, the brothers built the steam and hydroelectric generating station at the present site of Moores Park Dam. After being acquired by the Michigan Power Company, the dam was sold in 1919 to the city of Lansing and the hydroelectric generating station became part of the Lansing Board of Water and Light system. The dam still produces hydroelectric power to this day. (Caterino/CADL.)

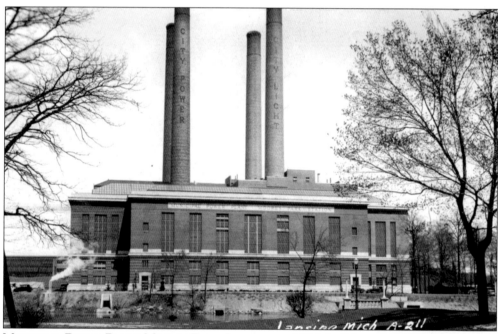

MUNICIPAL POWER PLANT MOORES PARK STATION, C. 1926. In February of 1922, construction began on the Moores Park (Eckert) Station on nine acres of land donated by the General Motors Corporation. The building was completed in 1926. In order to keep pace with the growing needs of the Lansing community, the plant has undergone several re-buildings throughout its history.

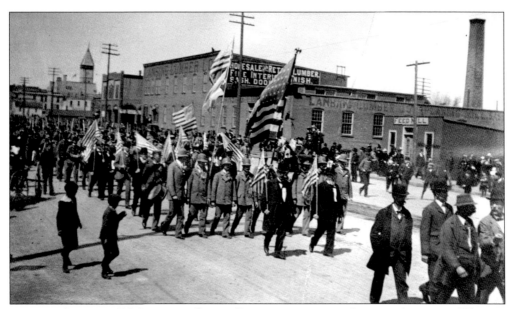

LANSING COMPANY E MARCHING OFF TO PARTICIPATE IN THE SPANISH-AMERICAN WAR ON APRIL 26, 1898. The Company was sent in January 1899 to Cienfuegos in Cuba, where they lost 14 men to yellow fever. This photograph shows the men marching east on Michigan Avenue to the train depot. The clock tower of city hall can be seen in the background. The parade is being led by the Lansing Police Department wearing English Bobbie style hats. (FPML/CADL.)

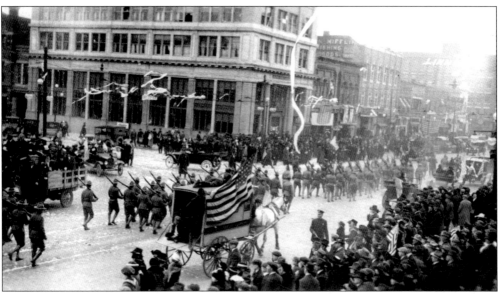

THE RETURN OF "LANSING'S OWN" 119TH FIELD ARTILLERY REGIMENT FROM THEIR SERVICE IN WORLD WAR I. The 630 soldiers of the unit were greeted with a hero's welcome they well deserved for service in the "War to End All Wars." On Tuesday May 13, 1919, thousands of Lansing residents gathered to welcome the returning soldiers. There were several emotional reunions as parents rushed out to embrace their soldier sons while the regiment marched down Washington Avenue. The parade was led by Lansing resident and commanding officer of the regiment Col. Chester B. McCormick. (FPML/CADL.)

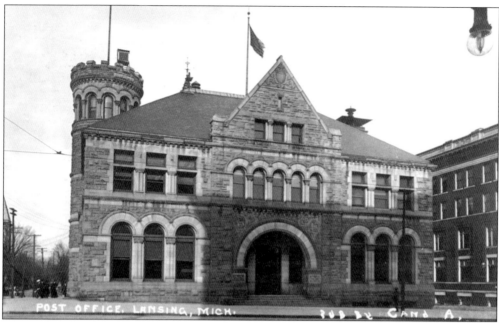

POST OFFICE, LANSING, MICHIGAN, C. 1910. Occupied in 1894, the post office was located on the corner of Capitol and Michigan Avenues, site of the present day city hall. The Lansing Post Office became a first class office on May 9, 1901, on the basis of gross receipts. In 1906, the post office made four business and two residential deliveries daily. First-class postage was 2¢ and post cards were 1¢.

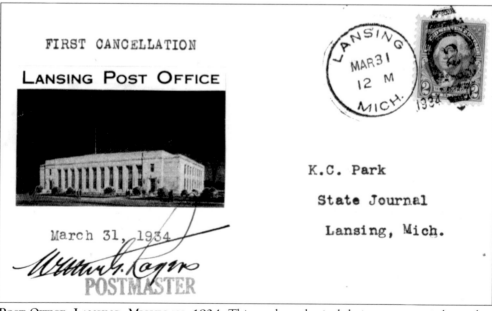

POST OFFICE, LANSING, MICHIGAN, 1934. This modern classical design structure is located at 315 West Allegan and faces the State Capitol. Bowd and Munson, local architects, designed the building with Albert Kahn Company, Inc., as consultants. This envelope, signed by Postmaster Walter G. Rogers, commemorates the opening of the new post office on March 31, 1934.

Five

TRANSPORTATION

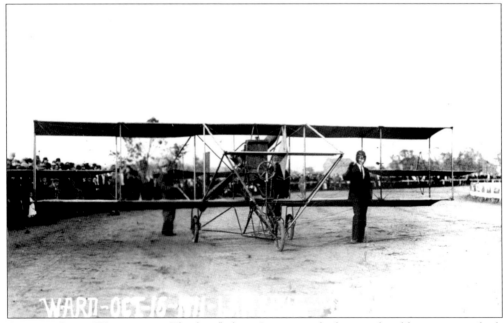

AVIATOR JIMMY WARD, 1911. The first flight in Lansing took place on the old racecourse, which is now the Red Cedar Golf Course, on October 15, 1911. Beter than 20,000 people packed the grandstands to watch Jimmy Ward perform stunts with his Curtiss biplane, the "Shooting Star."

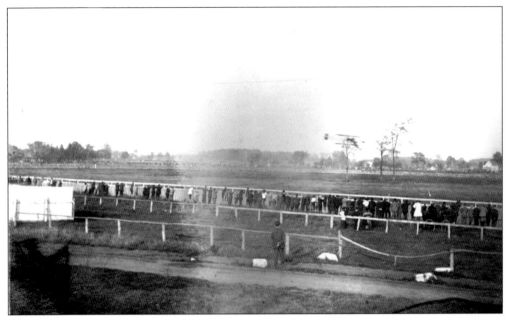

A Previously Unseen Photograph of Jimmy Ward's Aerial Demonstration at the Old Racecourse. As the headlines the next day proclaimed, "Ward makes flights that thrill large crowd of people. Thousands cheer as Jimmy soars through the air." (FPML/CADL.)

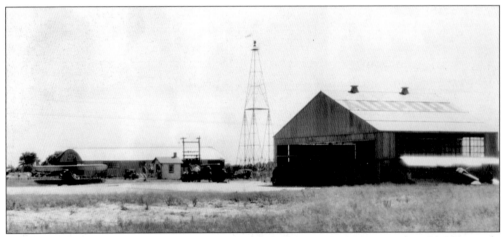

Capital City Airport, 1928. On the weekend of July 14–15, 1928, more than 70,000 people witnessed the program of events for the dedication of the Capital City Airport. Noted Arctic explorer Capt. George Hubert Wilkins and his companion Lt. Carl B. Eielson were among the honored guests. An exhibition air show was held, featuring dozens of flyers including Art Davis of East Lansing and Eddie Preston of Lansing. Six planes from the Selfridge field performed along with members of the 107th Observation Squadron, Michigan National Guard.

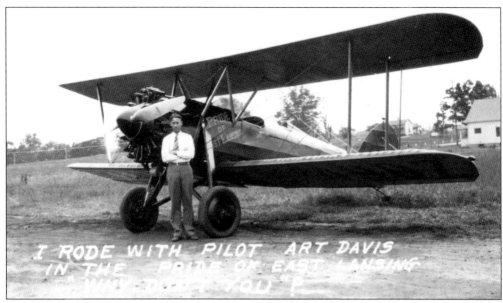

ART DAVIS AND HIS SPIRIT OF EAST LANSING, C. 1928. Art Davis is Lansing's best known flying son. He launched his aeronautical career during World War I and gained such skill that he won more race trophies and first place prizes in closed course racing than any other pilot in the world. Art Davis successfully managed to create his own path in aviation turning barnstorming, exhibition flying, and racing into a career. Davis worked with the best of the Lansing aviators including Bob O'Dell, Roger Don Rae, Clem Sohn, and Charlie Zmuda, among others.

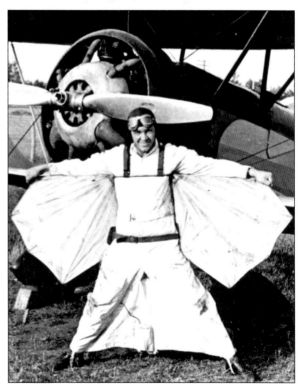

CHARLIE ZMUDA, THE "BAT MAN," 1938. Clem Sohn, Lansing's first "Bat Man"—so-called because of "bat-wings" that he wore to direct his fall through space, died in 1937 during an air show event in Paris, France. Sohn's parachute failed to open. A memorial plaque is located in Eastern High School. The second "Bat Man" to take to the skies, with the Art Davis Air Show was Charlie Zmuda. Zmuda would leap from a plane at 10,000 feet and soar through the air on his wings, use smoke to mark his flight and then open his parachute for landing, thrilling crowds around the globe. (Caterino/CADL.)

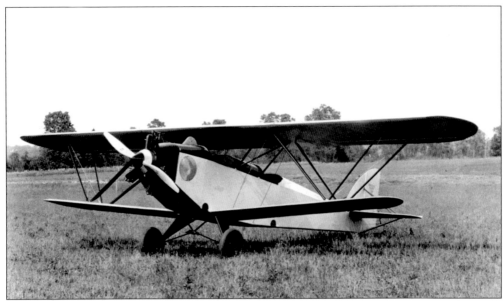

DRIGGS DART II, C. 1930s. In 1927, the Driggs Aircraft Co. was organized for the manufacture of the Driggs Dart and Skylark aeroplanes. The officers of the company included Harry F. Harper, president; Ivan H. Driggs, vice-president and general manager; E.C. Shields, secretary, and Hugo B. Lundberg as treasurer. Their offices were located at 2301 West Saginaw. The company ceased operations in 1932.

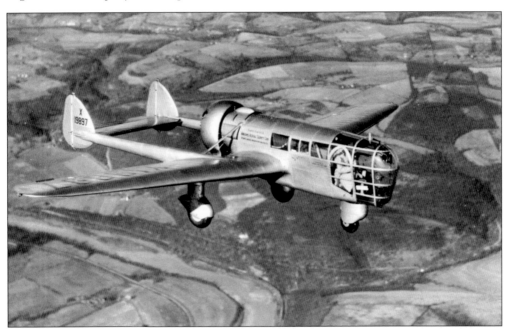

ABRAMS EXPLORER, C. LATE 1930s. Talbert Abrams founded the Abrams Aircraft Corporation to manufacture a photographic aircraft. The airplane known as the Abrams Explorer was built for the sole purpose of aerial photography. The plane featured a glass nose, twin tail booms, a pusher engine, and tricycle landing gear. The Explorer was in use until 1948 when Abrams donated the aircraft to the Smithsonian Institution in Washington, D.C.

LANSING AVIATION CLUB, 1932. Aviator John Matthews is pictured instructing Maynard Hill, reporter for the *State Journal*, on the finer points of flying for his 1932 newspaper series *Learning to Fly*. John Matthews has penned on the back of the photograph, ". . .He (Maynard Hill) had just punched a runway grade stake thru an aileron on take-off. I had let him go a little too far before trying to correct him. We were flying on the field while it was undergoing a WPA work project. He was at that dangerous stage where if he had been half as good as he thought he was he would have been twice as good as I was. He was quite deflated and soloed shortly after."

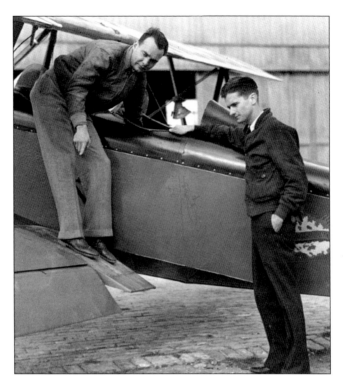

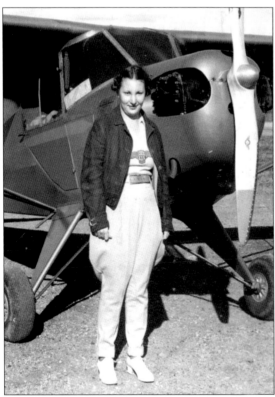

MARION "BABE" WEYANT, 1937. In 1931 at the age of 13, Babe took her first plane ride in a beautiful red Waco Taperwing with pilot Roger Don Rae and her great-grandfather, Eugene Olin. During 1934, she set up a refreshment stand at the airport to be close to the activity and raise money for flying lessons. Babe soloed, at the age of 18, in an Aeronca owned by Harvey M. Hughes. She received her private pilot's license in 1937. In 1946, she married Dale C. Ruth. Today, Babe continues to be active in aviation circles. She shares her memories of those early days of her aviation career. In 1988 she was enshrined in the Michigan Aviation Hall of Fame for her contributions to aviation as a pioneer woman aviator and historian. In 2002, the Ninety-Nines honored her with The Award of Achievement for her contributions. ("Babe" Weyant Ruth Collection)

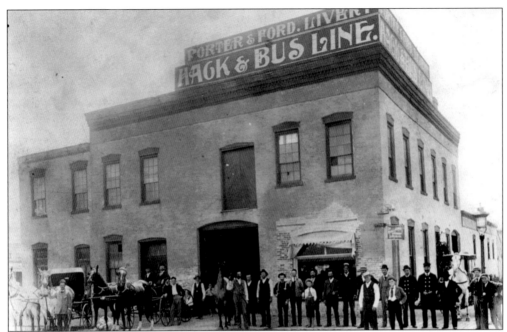

PORTER AND FORD LIVERY AS WELL AS THE HACK & BUS LINE WERE LOCATED AT 300 SOUTH CAPITOL AVENUE. The original structure was a foundry built just after the Civil War by Stannard and Luther Baker. In 1880 William Porter opened a livery stable in the building and operated a business that survived for 85 years. The livery stable closed in 1908 due to a fire and James Porter built a new building to serve as a service station and parking garage. The Porter family managed the business until 1965 when it was torn down and replaced by the Commerce Center Building, now the Cooley Law School Building. (FPML/CADL.)

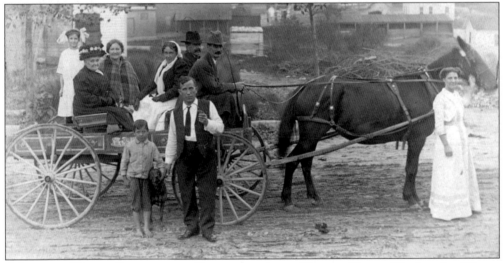

A LANSING WAGON LOADED WITH PASSENGERS FOR A TRIP TO TOWN. The Lansing Wagon Works was organized in 1881 and located on North Grand Street, between Shiawassee and Genesee Streets, with two blocks frontage and extending to the river. In 1902 the officers included F. Thoman, president, E.F. Cooley, secretary and treasurer, and J.A. Meyers, manager. About 150 men were employed, producing nearly 8,000 vehicles annually.

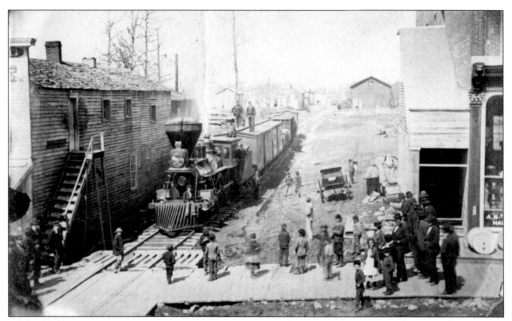

LS&MS Railroad in North Lansing, c. 1870. This scene shows an early steam locomotive and freight cars sitting on the tracks in North Lansing at Franklin (now Grand River) Avenue. Children and residents have gathered, with one young lad taking advantage of the moment by sitting on the "cow-catcher." The storefront to the right is that of A.N. Hart, custom and merchant miller, and also a dealer in hardware and groceries. (MSU Archives and Historical Collections.)

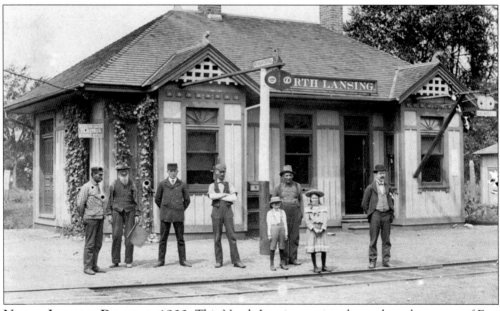

North Lansing Depot, c. 1900. This North Lansing station, located on the corner of East and Franklin (now Grand River) Avenue served both the Michigan Central (Saginaw Branch) and the Pere Marquette Railroads. In 1904, F.G. Smith is listed as the ticket agent and George W. French as freight agent. The individuals depicted in this photograph are unidentified.

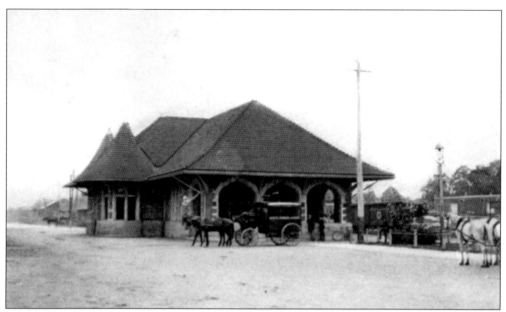

UNION STATION, C. 1905. The Union Station depot, located at 637 East Michigan Avenue, opened for business in June of 1902. The depot served both the Michigan Central and Pere Marquette Railroad lines with four trains traveling each way everyday except Sunday. In addition, Lansing received 26 daily mail trains. The handsome structure, depicted here with a horse-drawn coach awaiting passengers, was designed by Spiers and Rohns of Detroit. Passenger service to Lansing was discontinued in 1972. Today the building houses a restaurant, Clara's Lansing Station.

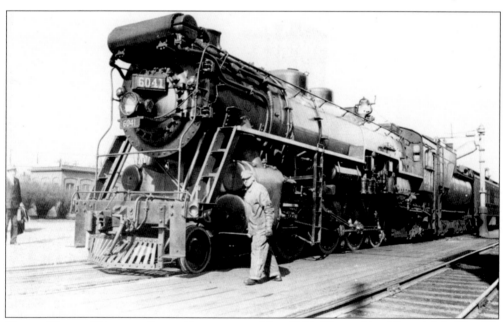

GRAND TRUNK WESTERN STEAM LOCOMOTIVE NO. 6041. Pictured is a Type 4-8-2, Class U-1-c locomotive built by Baldwin in 1925. It was known as the *Inter-City Limited* with Howard Williams as its engineer. The total engine weight was 354,100 pounds. This photograph was taken on the tracks in Lansing, 1929.

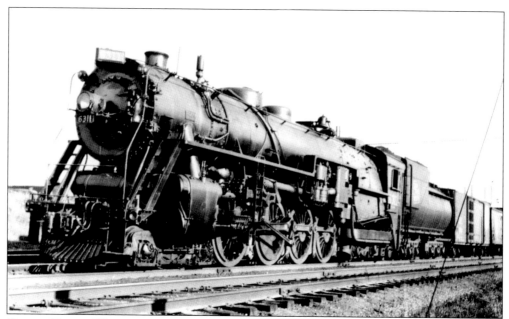

GRAND TRUNK WESTERN STEAM LOCOMOTIVE NO. 6311. Pictured, is a Type 4-8-4, Class U-3-a locomotive built by the American Locomotive Company, 1929. Its total engine weight was 399,000 pounds. It is pictured on the tracks in Lansing, 1932.

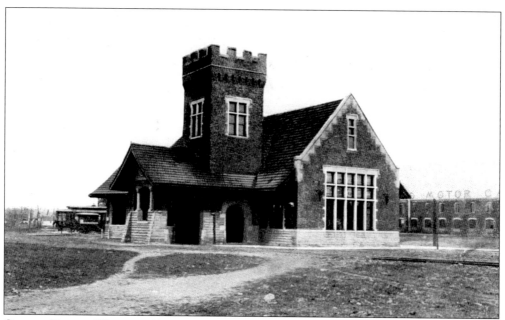

GRAND TRUNK WESTERN DEPOT, C. 1910. This passenger station located at 1203 South Washington opened in January, 1903. The REO Motor Car Company factory is visible to the right of the depot. In the early years, passengers awaiting trains were entertained by the automobiles being driven on the REO test track which lay south of the depot. A streetcar and horse-drawn hack can be seen at the left. Unlike many of Lansing's historic buildings which have been demolished throughout the years, this depot still stands, awaiting its uncertain future.

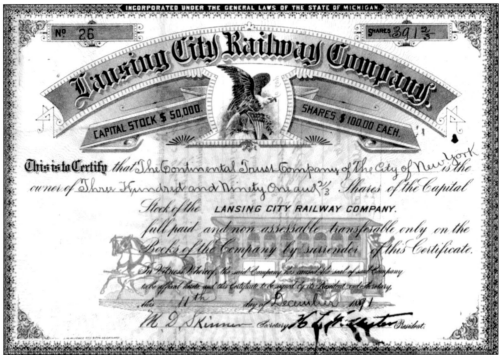

LANSING CITY RAILWAY COMPANY STOCK CERTIFICATE, 1891. The Lansing City Railway was Lansing's first horse-car line, operating from 1886 to 1890. Two horse-drawn trolley car routes were in operation serving Franklin (now Grand River) Avenue from Clark Street to Washington Avenue, then south to the Grand Trunk Depot and on Michigan Avenue from the State Capitol to Union Station. During 1890, the horses were retired and the company converted to an electric line. This stock certificate features a vignette of a horse-drawn trolley car.

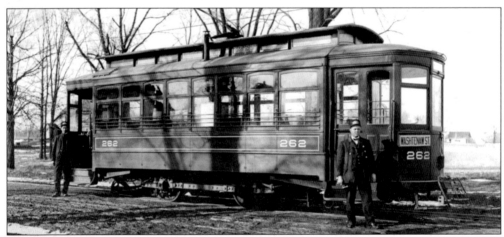

WASHTENAW STREET STREETCAR NO. 262, C. 1910–1920. These two motormen (unidentified) have taken a brief break from their schedule to pose in front of their streetcar. From the organization of the Lansing City Railway Company to the end of the streetcar era, several companies served the transportation needs of the citizens including the Michigan Railway Company, Michigan United Railways Company, and the Michigan Electric Railway Company. Bus transportation would replace travel by streetcar in the 1930s.

Six

COMMUNITY

THE SIMPLE GRACE OF ONE OF
LANSING'S EARLIEST CHURCHES.
The First Baptist church of Lansing
was dedicated in October 1859 and
located on the southwest corner of
Washington Avenue and Ionia
Street. The land was deeded to the
church by the state in exchange for
property held by the Baptist church
at the southwest corner of
Washtenaw and Townsend. The
church was built between 1855 and
1859 at a cost of $5,000 and
remained in service until the
construction of the new church in
1894. Prior to the construction of
the First Baptist Church, services
were held in a sitting room at the
Franklin Street tavern; baptisms
were performed in the Grand River
at the foot of Ottawa Street. The
house to the left is the home of the
Stebbins family. (FPML/CADL.)

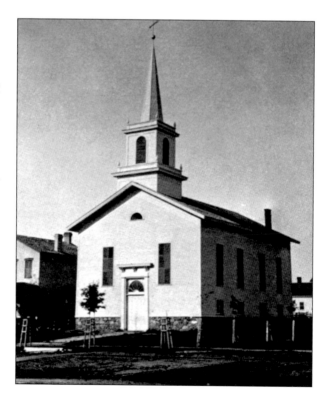

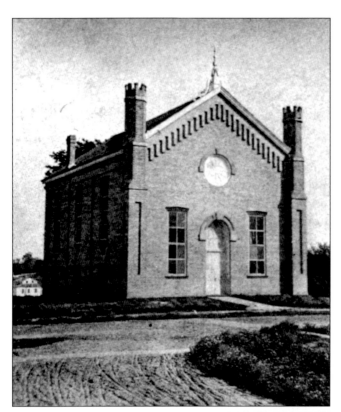

THE UNIVERSALIST CHURCH ON THE SOUTHEAST CORNER OF GRAND AND ALLEGAN STREETS, C. 1870S. Construction of this church began in 1859 on property that was a gift from the state legislature. The total cost of the structure was $6,000, and it was dedicated on October 24, 1863. It served the needs of its members until 1896 when it was deemed inadequate for the size of the congregation. The building was sold in January 1896 for $4,000 and a new church was built on Capitol Avenue. (FPML/CADL.)

THE FIRST PRESBYTERIAN CHURCH LOCATED ON THE CORNER OF ALLEGAN AND CAPITOL AVENUE. Constructed in 1887, the First Presbyterian Church was recognized as one of Lansing's historic landmarks. It was built of Marshall stone with a soaring steeple that dominated the skyline. In the background is Plymouth Congregational Church. The Presbyterian Church building was sold to the R.E. Olds Company in 1945 and demolished in 1948. Today a parking structure is on the site. (FPML/CADL.)

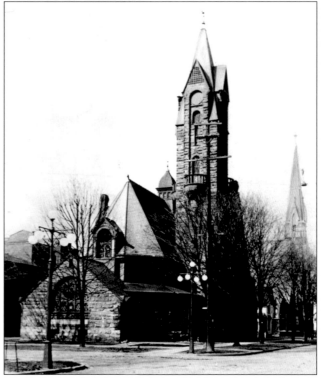

THE SOARING SPIRE OF PLYMOUTH CONGREGATIONAL CHURCH WAS A FIXTURE OF THE LANSING SKYLINE SINCE THE 1870S. In the late 1860s, the membership of the Congregational Chapel realized they were quickly outgrowing the confines of their facility, so in 1866 Cortland B. Stebbins was empowered to purchase the site at the corner of Allegan and Townsend, just across from the Capitol. The Congregational Chapel moved there in 1871 and in 1876 construction of a new church began. On March 16, 1877, the church was dedicated and over 1,200 people attended the ceremony. The total cost of construction was $18,000. Unfortunately, the church burned in a massive fire in February, 1971. (FPML/CADL.)

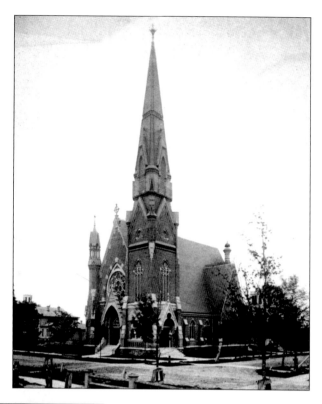

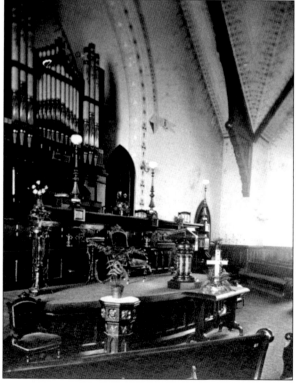

AN INTERIOR VIEW OF PLYMOUTH CONGREGATIONAL CHURCH, 1877. The Gothic Revival church with a spire that reached 160 feet was considered by Elijah Myers, the architect of the Michigan State Capitol, as one of the finest church structures in North America. Visible in the photograph is the Kilgen organ, produced by the Kilgen Organ Company of Saint Louis, Missouri, which sold organs to hundreds of churches, the most famous being St. Patrick's Cathedral in New York City. Plymouth Congregational Church was also known for the works of one of its ministers, Dr. Edwin W. Bishop, who served the church from 1918–1939. Dr. Bishop was a nationally recognized minister whose sermons were distributed across the nation. He also served as Chairman of the Ingham County Red Cross Chapter and compiled a report on the emergency response to the Bath Disaster. (FPML/CADL.)

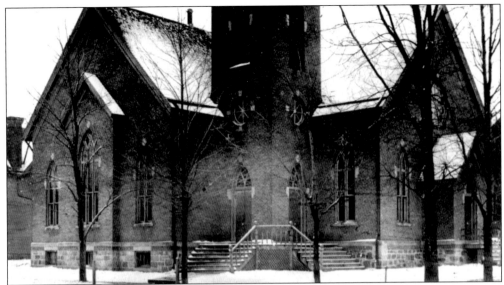

THE FREE WILL BAPTIST CHURCH, WAS LOCATED ON THE SOUTHEAST CORNER OF CAPITOL AVENUE AND KALAMAZOO STREET. The current site of the Capitol Area District Library's Main Library. Dedicated on November 16, 1884, the new church cost $9,000 to build. The church had an audience room, which measured 44 by 66 feet, and a vestry that was 24 by 40 feet. The pews were made of black walnut and ash, purchased from a firm in Richmond, Indiana. In 1905, due to dwindling membership, the building was sold to the Odd Fellows to serve as their new lodge, Capital Lodge No. 45. The church was torn down in the 1920s and a gas station occupied the site. The last remnant of the Baptist presence was removed in 1962 with the demolition of the parsonage house at 119 West Kalamazoo, which is visible in the extreme left of the photograph. (FPML/CADL.)

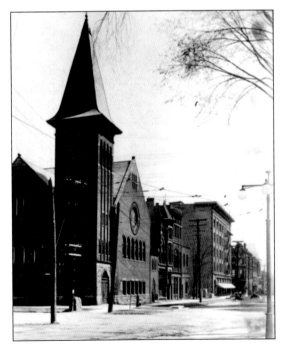

THE FIRST UNIVERSALIST CHURCH AT THE CORNER OF CAPITOL AVENUE AND OTTAWA STREET. In 1895, Sarah E.V. Emery donated the site for the new Universalist Church to the congregation and the church was constructed at a cost of $17,000. The church was sold to Lee Cahill in 1939–1940 for $24,750, and served as an office building until 1960 when the new Lansing Business University Building replaced it. In the background, the Tussing building is visible where Darius Moon once had an office; also visible is the home of the Lansing Woman's Club, and the offices of the Michigan Commercial Insurance Company. (FPML/CADL.)

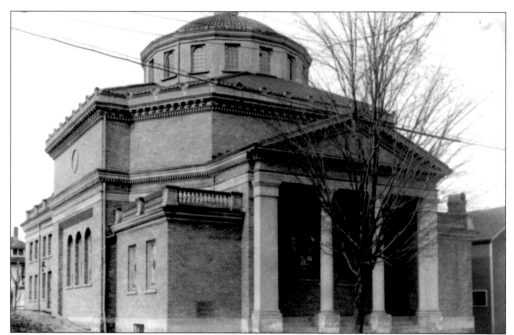

MAIN STREET METHODIST CHURCH WAS BUILT IN 1906 UNDER THE SUPERVISION OF REV. GEORGE GILLETT AT A COST OF $18,000. The most striking aspect of the building is its resemblance to the Pantheon in Rome. The church was lit by natural light, which flooded the auditorium from three sides through the dome. The building's architects were White & Hussey. The church was sold in 1961 to the Catholic Diocese of Lansing and in 1966 it was torn down because of the construction of I-496. (FPML/CADL.)

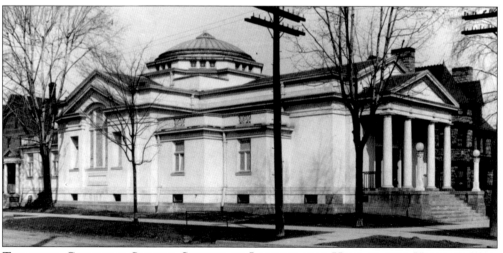

THE FIRST CHRISTIAN SCIENCE SERVICE IN LANSING WAS HELD IN THE HOME OF MRS. JENISON AT 621 WEST IONIA IN 1897. In 1907 a building fund was initiated to raise funds for the purchase of a site on the corner of Walnut and Allegan Streets. The cornerstone for the new building was laid on September 10, 1910, and less than a year later on May 10, 1911, the building was completed at a cost of $20,000. The facility was built to seat 450 people and an Austin organ was provided by Mrs. Schuetz in July, 1911. Mr. S.S. Berman from Chicago was the architect of the church. The site was purchased by the state of Michigan in 1946. (FPML/CADL.)

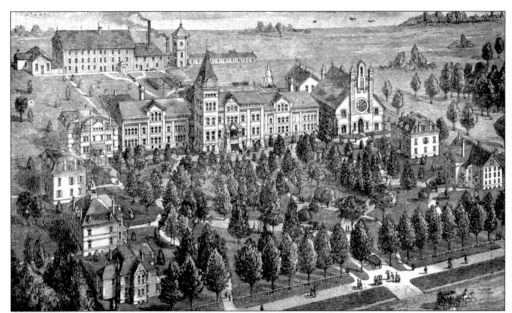

INDUSTRIAL SCHOOL FOR BOYS, C. 1870S. On February 10, 1855, the state legislature passed an appropriation for $25,000, "to locate a convenient site of at least 20 acres for a House of Correction for Juvenile Offenders." Lansing residents would donate 30 acres and the State purchased an additional 195 acres. Boys were committed to this institution for truancy or other offences and would remain until the age of 17 or 18. They were not sentenced for a definite time, but once committed to the school, all relatives, parents, and guardians lost all control of them. Boys were required to be in school four and one-half hours each day and work the same length of time in one of many trades.

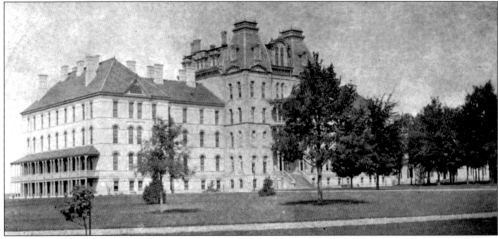

THE MICHIGAN SCHOOL FOR THE BLIND. This building was originally constructed as the Michigan Female College and was later sold to the Michigan Grand Lodge of Odd Fellows in 1871. In 1880 the state leased the site for the Odd Fellows to serve as the Michigan School for the Blind. In 1871 the state accepted a proposal by the Odd Fellows to transfer the 45 acres of the Odd Fellow's Institute to the state of Michigan, if the state would cancel the existing $10,000 mortgage. On the back of this photograph is a notation concerning the photographer: "Photograph by an amateur 14 years of age. Frank Godfrey 1889." (Caterino/CADL.)

LANSING HIGH SCHOOL BUILT IN 1874–1875 WITH A $50,000 BOND APPROVED BY THE CITIZENS OF LANSING. The architect was E.E. Myers. The bond was eventually paid off in 1905 with a final cost of $140,000. In the 1910s the upper floors were removed and the building modernized. When Eastern High School was built in the 1920s, the school was renamed Central High School. The building stands today as part of Lansing Community College and is remembered fondly as Old Central. The photograph is from 1901. (FPML/CADL.)

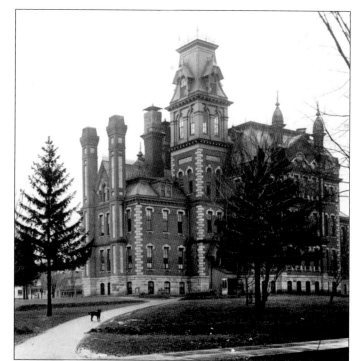

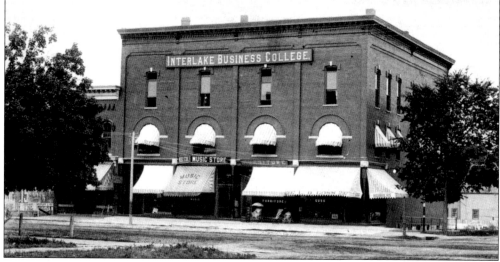

THE INTERLAKE BUSINESS COLLEGE LOCATED AT 231–237 SOUTH WASHINGTON AVENUE. Henry P. Bartlett and E.P. Holbrook founded the first business college in Lansing in 1867 in the old Benton House on South Washington. At one point the college was housed in the old state capitol building, the business was sold to the Johnson brothers who changed the name from Bartlett's Business College to Interlake Business College. The school was sold in 1898 to Hobart Beck, who expanded the college to encompass the entire third floor of 231–237 South Washington Avenue. Interlake Business College would become Lansing Business University, which was incorporated in 1908 and absorbed its major competitor, Central Michigan Business University. Lansing Business University later purchased Lansing Commercial Institute in 1914. The building at 231 South Washington was destroyed by fire in 1991 and is now a parking lot. (FPML/CADL.)

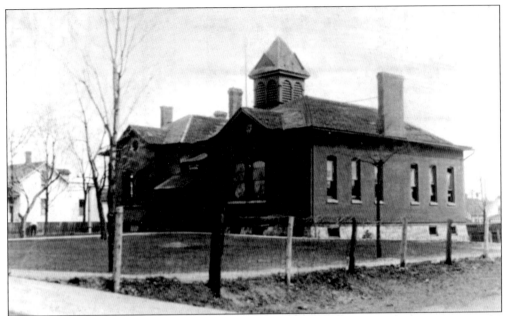

THE SOUTH STREET SCHOOL LOCATED AT 213 EAST SOUTH STREET. Constructed *c.* 1867 by Mr. Gillette as a two-room brick building, each room could accommodate 50 students. In May of 1892 an addition was added to the school at a cost of $2,300. The building was declared surplus in 1914 and served as a warehouse for Christman Co. until it was razed in 1964. (FPML/CADL.)

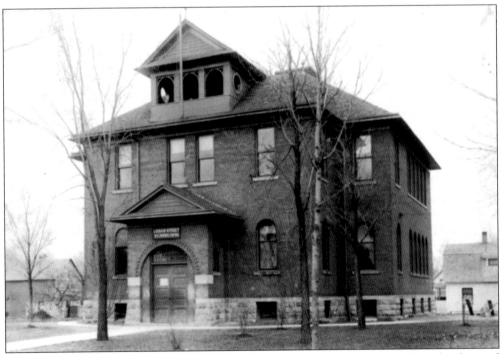

THE LOGAN STREET SCHOOL COMPLETED IN 1897 AT A COST OF $3,250. The school served the needs of the local community until it was closed 1933. The site was cleared in 1936 to make way for a more modern school. (FPML/CADL.)

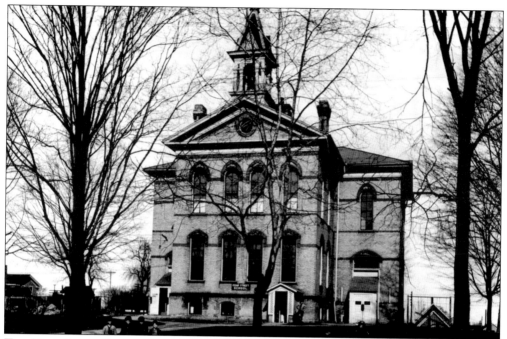

THE NEW CEDAR STREET SCHOOL. Located at 1100 North Cedar Street, the school was built to replace the original school on this site, which was severely damaged by fire in 1868. The new school was constructed in 1875 at a cost of $6,457. In 1917 the growing population of Lansing compelled the enlargement of the building at a cost of $49,000. By 1941 the old part of the second Cedar School was declared unsafe and it was razed, which was too bad because the old belfry lent an air of charm to the building. (FPML/CADL.)

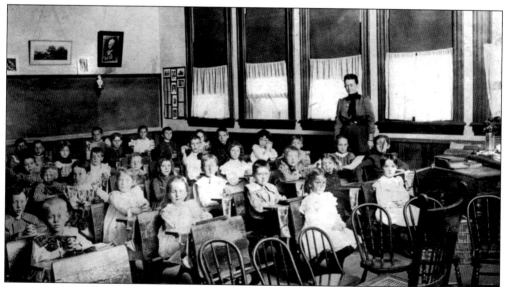

FIRST AND SECOND GRADES AT THE CHERRY STREET SCHOOL IN SEPTEMBER 1900. Although the names of the students are unknown, the teacher in the background is identified as Miss Waldo. The Cherry Street School still stands today and currently functions as an office for an architectural firm. (FPML/CADL.)

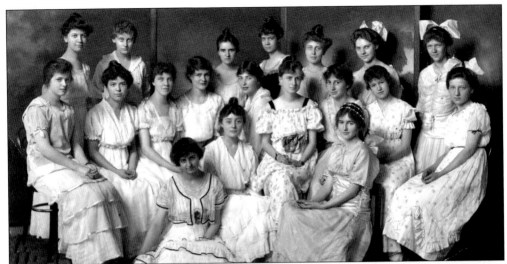

THE LOVELY YOUNG LADIES OF LANSING HIGH SCHOOL'S LAMBDA RHO TAU SORORITY IN 1914. Today fraternities, sororities, and other secret societies are prohibited by state law from operating in public high schools, but in 1914 this was not the case. (FPML/CADL.)

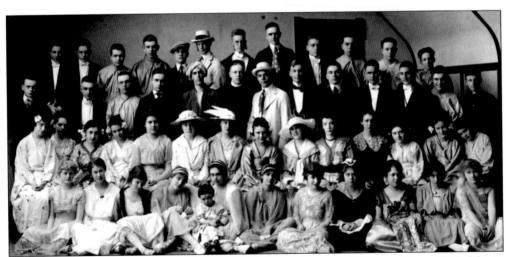

THE JUNIOR EXHIBITION BY THE CLASS OF 1918 PERFORMED THE PLAY THE MOON MAID. Written and directed by Miss Mary Derby of Lansing High School, the play is about Stanley Graham, an American painter in Japan who falls in love with his Japanese model, Tern San. The play was a love story complete with tragic misunderstandings, songs and dances by Geisha girls, and a happy ending. The play was performed at the Gladmer Theater on March 23, 1917, and was, as the *Oracle* yearbook describes ". . . pronounced a grand success by everyone who attended it." (Caterino/CADL.)

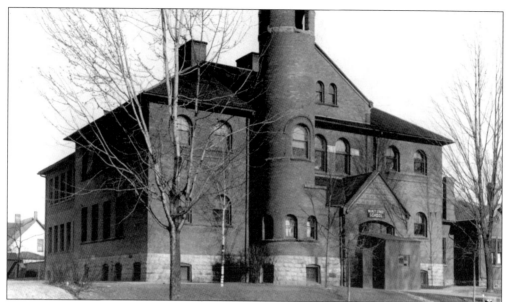

THE WALNUT STREET SCHOOL. The building was constructed in 1891 at 1020 North Walnut at a cost of $8,250. The original building consisted of four classrooms and was enlarged in 1905 with a four-room addition. In 1930 the school district decided to concentrate all the students in the district with special needs in one school and the Walnut Street facility was chosen. With the aid of the Federal Emergency Administration of Public Works an addition was made to the building in 1937. The addition added 16 new rooms to serve the special needs students. (FPML/CADL.)

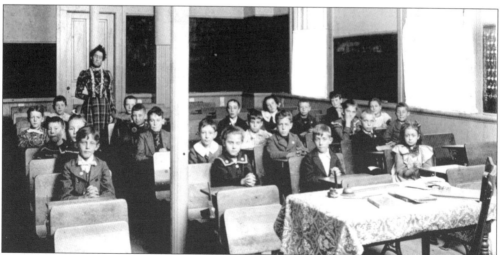

THE FOURTH GRADE CLASS OF THE TOWNSEND STREET SCHOOL IN SEPTEMBER 1900. Miss Moots is the teacher, and the students are identified as follows: (front row) Bertch, Brooks, Yarley, Peez, and Brumm; (second row) Schuber, Olds, Dudley, Keith, and Avery; (third row) Pitt, Guinn, Pattengill, and Stables; (fourth row) Albright, Holt, Teller, Long, and Maltry; (back row) Muller, Titus, and Burnett. The Townsend Street School served as an educational institution until 1928 when it became the home of the Board of Education. The building would later serve as the headquarters of the 46th Infantry Division of the Michigan National Guard. The structure was torn down in 1956. (FPML/CADL.)

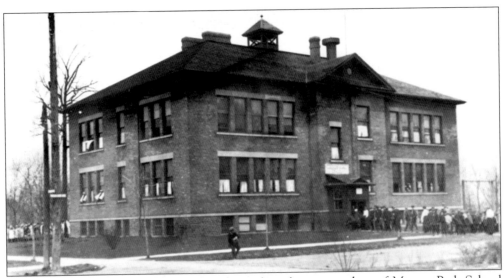

MOORES PUBLIC SCHOOL. The hardest thing about being a student of Moores Park School must have been the location of the nearby pool on warm days. The school was built in 1906 and designed by J.N. Churchill; the building originally consisted of just four classrooms. A second story was added in 1910. The school faced Woodlawn Avenue, but that did little to alleviate the pain and suffering of the students once the Wesley Bentz-designed Moores Park Pool was built. The pool may have helped to maintain discipline in the school, since no child would want to stay after school on those warm days and miss a dip in the pool. The building was replaced in 1957 by the new Moores Park School. (FPML/CADL.)

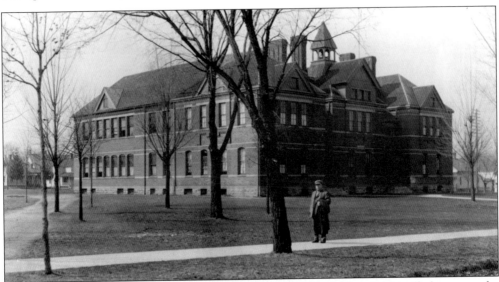

KALAMAZOO STREET SCHOOL, C. 1912. Constructed in 1883–1884 and originally known as the Clark School, the Kalamazoo Street School was one of the largest elementary schools in the city. Built at a cost of $11,000 and designed by the architect William Appleyard, the building originally had eight classrooms and, interestingly enough, a nearby frog pond needed to be filled to facilitate construction. In 1888 the name was changed to the Third Ward School, and in 1890 it was renamed the Kalamazoo Street School. The same year, the building was enlarged with a four-classroom addition and served the community until it was replaced in 1924. (FPML/CADL.)

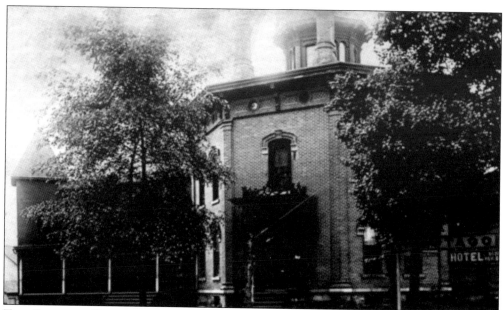

THE OCTAGON HOUSE, C. 1879. Built in 1854 by Lansing's first postmaster, Col. Whitney Jones, the Octagon House was one of Lansing's oddest residences. Located at 401 South Washington Avenue, the house was purchased in 1902 by Frank Arbaugh for the site of his new department store. The home was moved from Washington Avenue and relocated east on Kalamazoo, just behind Arbaugh's Department Store. The building was torn down in 1929–1930 to increase the store's parking. (FPML/CADL.)

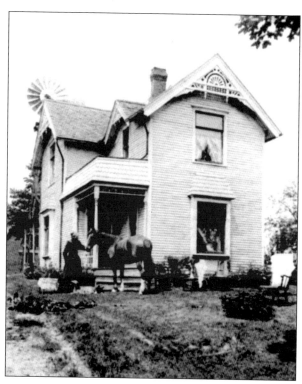

THE HOME OF JANE MCKAY AT 1829 EAST STREET IN 1906. Today we think of East Street as a part of urban Lansing, but in 1906 this was not the case. East Street was so named because it formed the eastern limit of the city. Little of East Street survives today. In 1870, it ran north from South Street to the city limits at North Street. Notice the windmill in the background; even in 1906 this was still a rural area within the city limits. (FPML/CADL.)

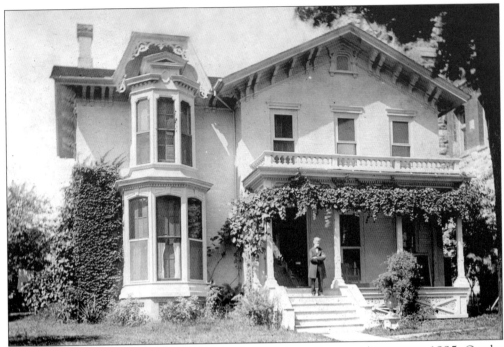

THE HOME OF CORTLAND B. STEBBINS AT 227 NORTH CAPITOL AVENUE IN 1895. On the porch is Cortland B. Stebbins, who lived in the home from 1865 to 1901. His daughter Susan would later reside there until 1935. (FPML/CADL.)

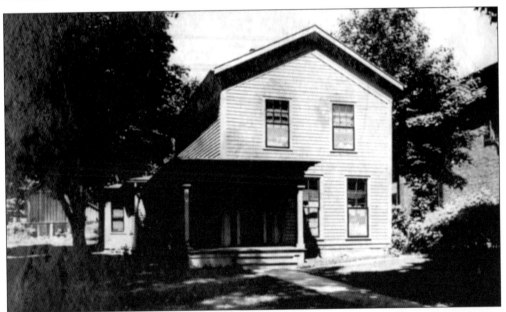

LOCATED AT 418 SOUTH WASHINGTON, THIS HOUSE WAS ONE OF THE FIRST COMMERCIAL BUILDINGS IN LANSING. Built in 1857 by J.B. Beebe, the building served as a hardware store, and after that, a tin shop. It was moved back from the street by E.H. Davis and converted into a residence. The home was later acquired by the Zimmerman family, who believed the building was once used as a post office. The house was razed in 1956. (FPML/CADL.)

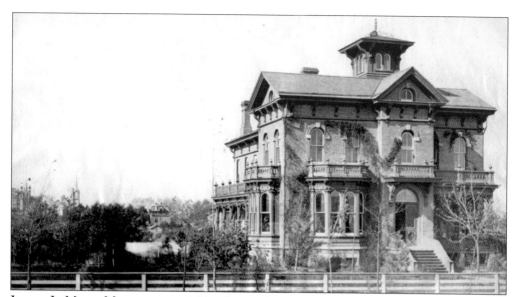

JAMES I. MEAD MUSEUM, C. 1870S. Located at 429 North Cedar Street, this beautiful mansion was built around 1870 for James I. Mead, one of Lansing's pioneer businessmen. The Mead residence served as one of the social centers of the emerging city. Mrs. Mead was active in social affairs and would entertain at the home. Following the death of Mr. Mead, the home was sold to the Lansing Women's Hospital Association, renovated and served as the City Hospital for a number of years until Edward W. Sparrow built the present Sparrow Hospital. Photo by C.H. Mead.

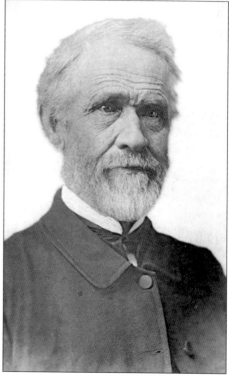

JAMES I. MEAD (1817–1888). One of Lansing's most remarkable businessmen, James I. Mead arrived in Detroit during the 1830s and moved to Lansing in 1852. His business enterprises included a dry goods store, saw mill, flour mill, and chair factory, as well as one of Lansing's first theaters, Mead's Hall. His son, Charles H. Mead, was an accomplished artist and captured many views of the growing capital city with his pen and camera.

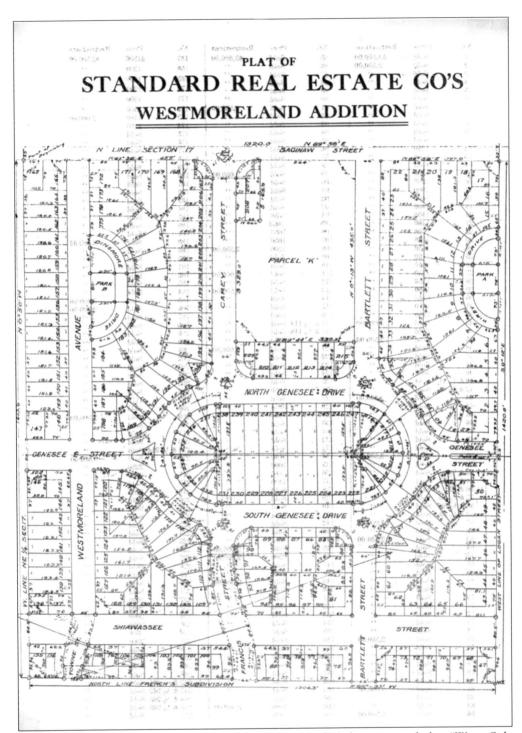

PLAT OF WESTMORELAND ADDITION, c. 1920s. Included as part of the "West Side Neighborhood" today, the Westmoreland addition is bound on the north by Saginaw Street, with lots running along Shiawassee Street on the south, Logan Street on the east, and Westmoreland on the west. Lots were originally priced from $880 to $3,500.

A HOME OF YOUR OWN

After all is said and done, the happiest man is the fellow who has a home of his own.

These fine, modern homes, SOLD ONLY TO REO employes, at prices ranging from $5,000 to $5,500.00—

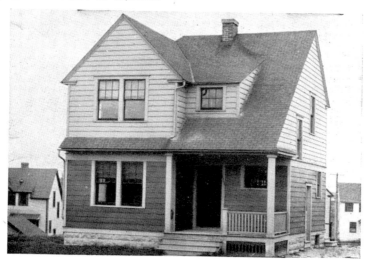

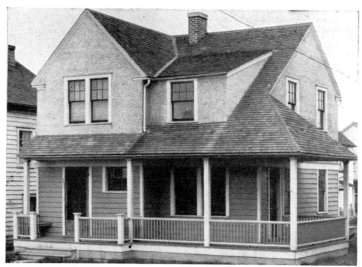

And All You Need to Pay Is
$300 (or more) down and
$40 (or more) per month.

Some of these REO houses have six rooms and bath, and some seven, with full basements.

Every REOITE Should AND CAN Own His Own Home.
Call at the Welfare Dept. for Information

REO HOME AD, MAY, 1925. The REO Motor Car Company promoted home ownership as a means of a stable workforce. South Lansing, in proximity of the REO factory, was known as "REO Town."

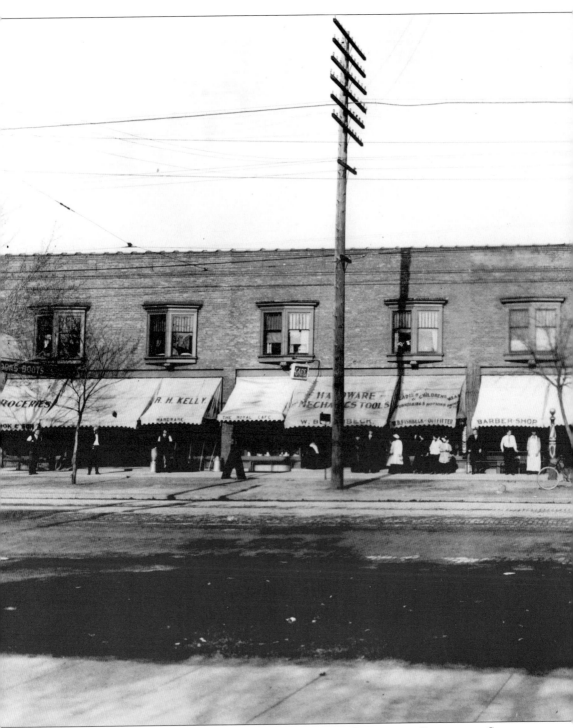

THE HEART OF ANY NEIGHBORHOOD WAS FOUND IN THE STORES AND SHOPS THAT SUPPORTED THE LOCAL RESIDENTS. The Sparrow block, 1133–1149 South Washington, was an example of this. Pictured here from left to right are the grocery store of Orin Cook, the jewelry store of E. Crawford, R.H. Kelly's hardware store, the Royal Café, the W. B. Fishbeck outfitter and tool store,

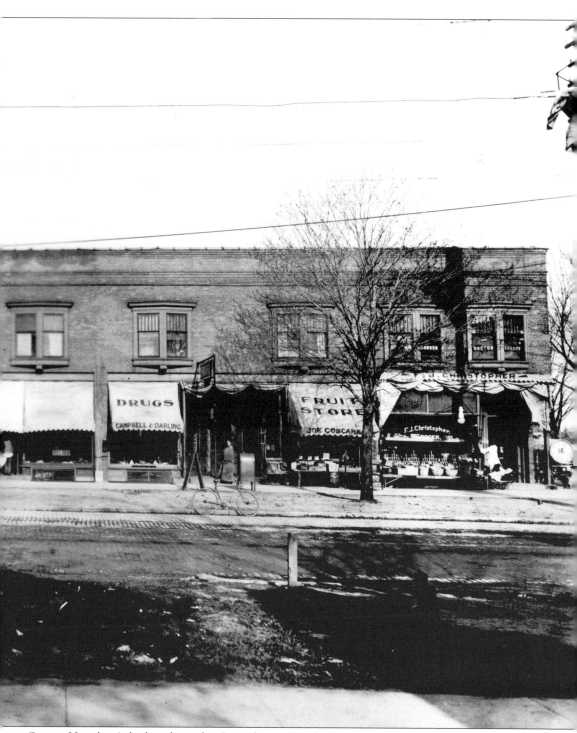

George Hamilton's barber shop, the Capitol Meat Market, Campbell & Darling Drugstore and postal substation, Joe Coscarelle's fruit market, and Christopher's grocery store. Above these businesses were the offices of doctors, dentists, and attorneys. The block had everything residents might need, and it was all within walking distance of their neighborhood. (FPML/CADL.)

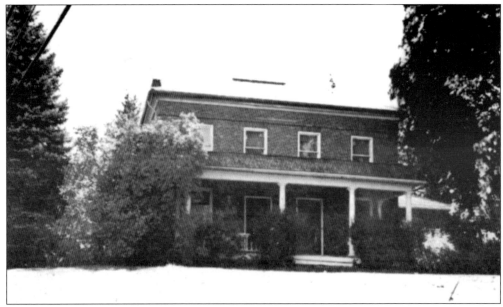

THE HOME OF HENRY H. NORTH, LOCATED AT 426 EAST NORTHRUP IN SOUTH LANSING. Henry North purchased the land for his home in 1839 and 1841 for the incredible price of $1.25 an acre. In 1854 he began construction of the brick home in the above photograph. The house had 11 rooms with five bedrooms, two bathrooms, a den, a dining room, and pine floors throughout. The most famous resident of the house was Doctor James Seymour North, the local country doctor. The home was razed in 1985, after the death of Marion North. (FPML/CADL.)

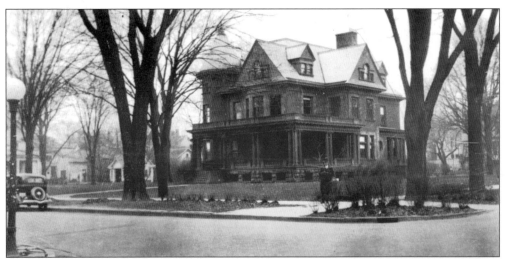

THE HOME OF J.H. MOORES AT 500 TOWNSEND STREET. Charles Maynard, a banker from Portland, Michigan, built this home in 1894. It was sold to Justice Joseph B. Moore in 1895. J.H. Moores acquired the home in 1904 when he retuned to Lansing. During his lifetime, J.H. Moores made and lost several fortunes but never forgot the debt he owed the city of Lansing. Moores donated 18 acres to the city, which became Moores Park. After his death in 1918, the house served as an apartment building, USO headquarters, and the home of the 500 Club. The YMCA acquired the home in the late 1920s for the site of their new building, but the Great Depression and World War II delayed construction. The house was torn down in 1948. (FPML/CADL.)

ARTHUR O. BEMENT RESIDENCE.
This home was built in 1876 by
Arthur O. Bement, the president of E.
Bement's and Sons, which was the
largest company in the city at that
time. The home at 310 South Grand
Avenue was considered by many to
have the most exquisite interior of any
residence in Lansing. It boasted five
chimneys and a tremendous amount
of oak in the floors and interior
woodwork. In the 1880s, South Grand
Avenue between Washtenaw and
Main Street was the finest residential
area in the city, and residents of the
area hosted numerous parties and
social events. Arthur O. Bement died
in 1926 and the residence was torn
down in 1939. (FPML/CADL.)

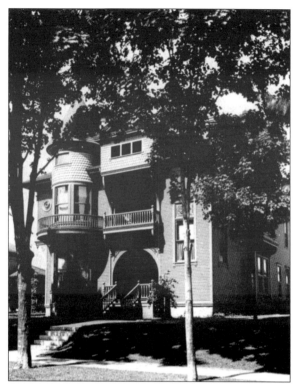

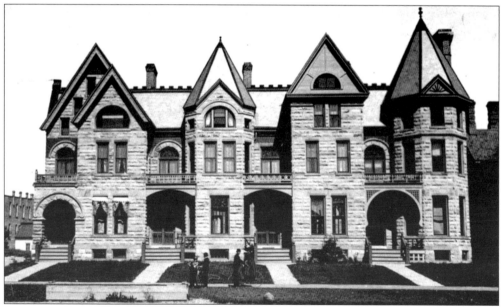

LOCATED CLOSE TO THE CAPITOL IN THE 200 BLOCK OF CAPITOL AVENUE. These
townhouses were built by O.M. Barnes in 1887 at a cost of $12,000. Their proximity to the state
Capitol made them the address of choice for many of the state's elite. Designed by architect
Claire Allen, the designer of the county courthouses in Van Buren, Hillsdale, and Shiawassee
counties, the four flats, as they were referred to, were quite attractive. They would be torn down
in 1925–1926 to make way for the new Masonic Temple. (FPML/CADL.)

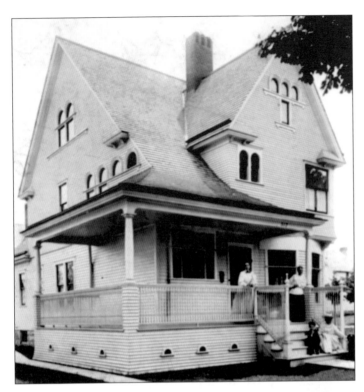

A Lovely View of the Home at 517 South Capitol in 1896. In the picture are E.M. Mastin, Clarence Roe, Roseanne Roe, and Carr the dog. The house was owned by Percy Mastin and is a wonderful example of the style of home present in Lansing at the turn of the century. The arched windows lend lightness to the home and the landscaping produced a clean and orderly appearance. (FPML/CADL.)

The B.F. Davis Mansion. Perhaps the best example of the opulent style of Victorian architecture with Eastlake ornamentation that ever graced the neighborhoods of Lansing. Built in 1889 at 528 South Washington and designed by Darius Moon, the mansion embodied

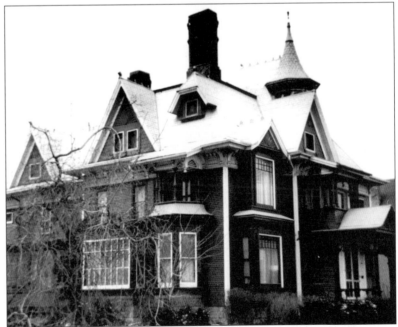

everything that a Victorian gentleman would require. The mansion had 17 rooms, elaborate interior woodwork, and several fire places. In 1971, the interception of the Greater Lansing Historical Society delayed its destruction. Unfortunately, the mansion was damaged by fire on February 29, 1972, and it was torn down in July of 1972. (FPML/CADL.)

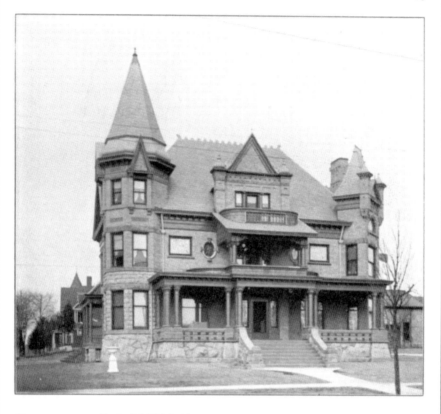

D. B. MOON, ARCHITECT.

ROOMS 5 & 6 DODGE BLOCK   Citizens' Phone 974

(R. E. OLDS' RESIDENCE, LANSING, MICH.)

I MAKE a specialty of plans for fine residences, and refer you to the following gentlemen as a few of the many for whom I have designed homes:—

E. W. Sparrow,	R. E. Olds,	H. D. Luce,	Henry Kositchek,
B. F. Davis,	J. A. Brooks,	F. L. Dodge,	Geo. H. Kneal,
J. Stahl,	H. M. Rogers,	Wm. A. Brown,	C. D. Woodbury,
Geo. Keith,	J. A. Bissinger,	A. C. Stebbins,	Geo. Wilson.

I keep duplicate prints of all plans sent out from my office, and can furnish them complete at a very low price. Come and look them over and you may find just what you want; you will certainly get some new ideas about modern buildings that will make you happy. I have a great variety of modern house plans, and will be pleased to show them at any time; it will cost you nothing to see them. Estimates given and all work guaranteed to be satisfactory in every respect.

RANSOM E. OLDS MANSION. This 1904 Lansing City Directory ad promotes the work of Darius B. Moon, architect, and features the residence of Ransom E. Olds. The Olds family home was located at 720 South Washington Avenue. In 1966, the home was demolished to allow for the construction of I-496 through the city.

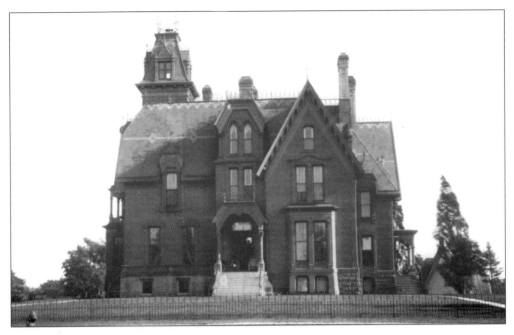

BARNES CASTLE. Once the epitome of Victorian architecture in Lansing, the Barnes mansion would suffer a tragic end. Built in 1875 for Orlando M. Barnes, a former mayor and railroad tycoon, the mansion was designed by L.D. Grosevenor. Built on three acres of land at the south end of Capitol Avenue and bordered by Main Street and Washington Avenue, the mansion sat 75 feet above the Grand River on a bluff. The gardens that surrounded the mansion were designed by landscape architect Adam Oliver and were considered the finest in the city. The home had 26 rooms, 14-foot-high ceilings, consisted of over 17,000 square feet, and was the meeting site for the political elite of the state. The mansion was acquired by the Lansing Parks Department and torn down in 1957 to build a parking lot. (FPML/CADL.)

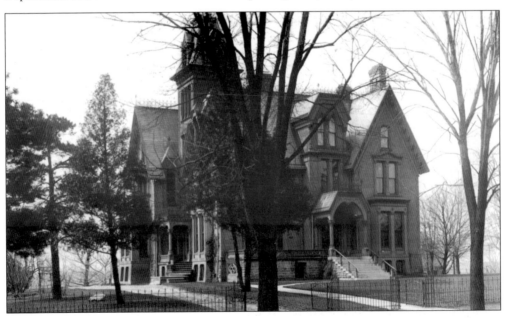

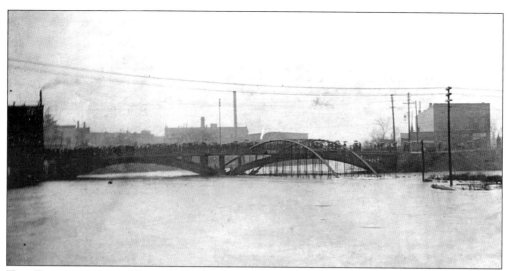

THE FLOOD OF 1904. If you look closely you can see the Kalamazoo Street Bridge wedged under the Michigan Avenue Bridge. The ironic aspect of the disaster was that the Kalamazoo Street Bridge was the original Michigan Avenue Bridge from 1871–1893 until it was replaced by the new Michigan Avenue Bridge in 1893. The steel structure of the bridge was then moved to Kalamazoo Street. After the flood, the Kalamazoo Street Bridge was salvaged and erected again at Kalamazoo Street, where it stood until its replacement in 1925. (FPML/CADL.)

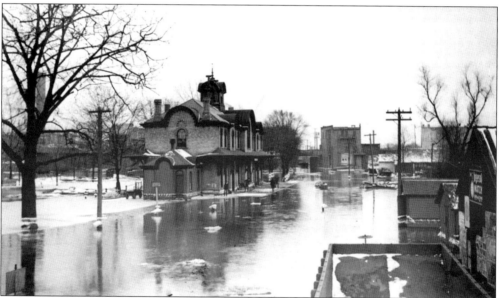

THE FLOOD OF 1904 NOT ONLY DESTROYED THE BRIDGES INTO LANSING, IT ALSO PREVENTED TRAINS FROM ENTERING THE LAKE SHORE AND MICHIGAN SOUTHERN DEPOT. The depot was built in 1868 and located on Condit Street just east of the Grand River and north of Michigan Avenue. The depot's proximity to the Grand River made it susceptible to flooding. The photograph shows the extent of the damage to the depot and the inability of trains to negotiate this stretch of tracks. A new depot was built further east on Michigan Avenue and the danger of a flood stopping all transportation into the city was decreased. The old depot was razed in 1938. (Caterino/CADL.)

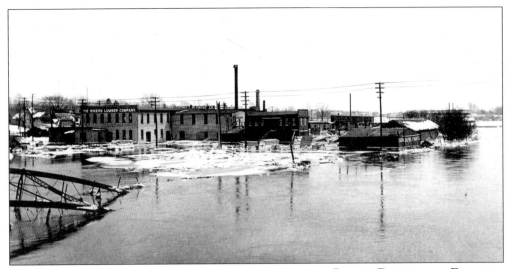

THE VIEW LOOKING SOUTH FROM THE MICHIGAN AVENUE BRIDGE DURING THE FLOOD OF 1904. In the foreground to the left, the structure of the Kalamazoo Street Bridge is visible. The Rickerd Lumber Company is the building just above the wreckage of the Kalamazoo Street Bridge. The flooding was so intense that the Rickerd Company built booms in order to keep lumber from floating away. In North Lansing, the Lansing Company failed to do this and their stock of lumber was washed away. (FPML/CADL.)

THE LOGAN STREET BRIDGE. The destruction of the Kalamazoo Street Bridge in the flood on 1904 is well known, but what is usually overlooked is the destruction of the Logan Street Bridge late in the day on March 25, 1904. This photograph shows the Logan Street Bridge on March 27, 1904. One section of the bridge became wedged under the Grand Trunk Railroad Bridge, while the other half crashed into the Piatt Powerhouse, near Moores Park Dam, demolishing the Powerhouse. The bridge was replaced later that year at a cost of $9,297. The other bridges washed away in the flood were the Cedar Street Bridge and the Mt. Hope Bridge. (Caterino/CADL.)

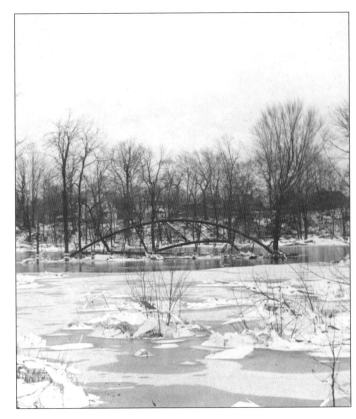

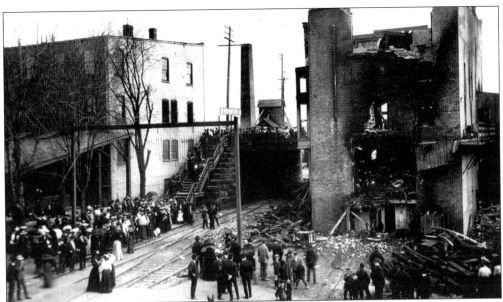

THE BRYAN HOTEL FIRE. Located at 327 Michigan Avenue, the Bryan Hotel, owned and operated by Rollo K. Bryan, was destroyed by fire in the early hours of April 29, 1904. The fire began the previous evening at around 9:30 p.m. and spread throughout the building. Mr. Bryan was described as a minister of sorts and a champion of the underdog. Beds were rented for 25¢ a night and even the basement was employed for accommodations. Four people died in the blaze, which was attributed to carelessness. (FPML/CADL.)

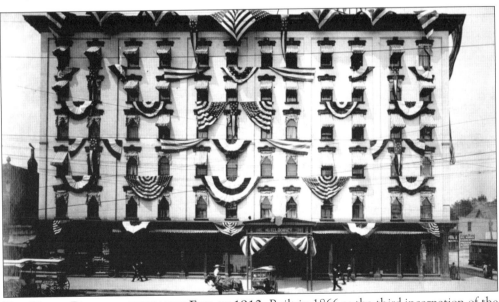

THE HOTEL DOWNEY BEFORE THE FIRE OF 1912. Built in 1866 as the third incarnation of the Lansing House, Henry Downey acquired this hotel in 1887 and he renamed it the Hotel Downey in 1888. The hotel was used as campaign headquarters in several gubernatorial campaigns. Suite 201 in the hotel became know as the "Victory Room" because of the list of successful gubernatorial candidates that occupied it. The Hotel Downey closed on May 1, 1936, and an era of Michigan political history ended. (FPML/CADL.)

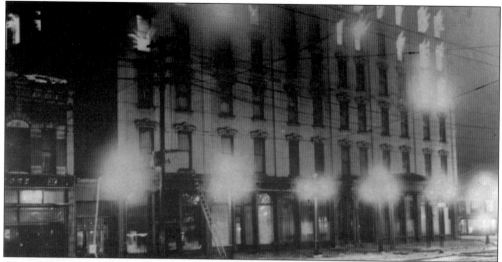

ON THE NIGHT OF FEBRUARY 6, 1912, THE HOTEL DOWNEY WAS DESTROYED BY FIRE. Losses were estimated at $109,991. The hotel had been expanded in 1907–1910 when two stories were added to the structure and the new sixth floor became a convention hall. After the fire, the building was quickly rebuilt because none of the exterior walls of the building had been damaged. However, it never again regained its place as a favorite Lansing watering hole. Photograph taken by George H. Bonnell. (FPML/CADL.)

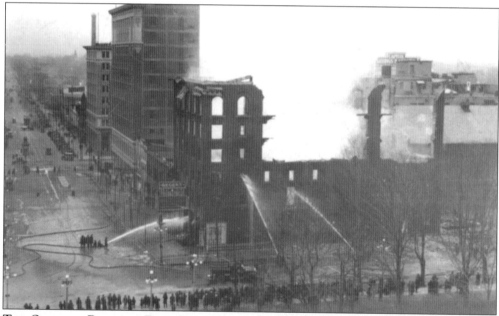

THE OAKLAND BUILDING FIRE. One of Lansing's oldest and largest structures was located at the corner of Capitol and Michigan Avenues, on the site of the current Romney Building. On the morning of Friday, December 22, 1923, fire swept through the structure. A milkman who was beginning his delivery route sounded the fire alarm at 5:10 a.m. By 7:45 a.m. Friday morning the flames were contained but the building was essentially gutted. Damage to the Oakland Building was estimated at $300,000. Fire Chief Hugo Delfs was of the opinion that the blaze began under the Regent Theater's stage and swept up through the building.

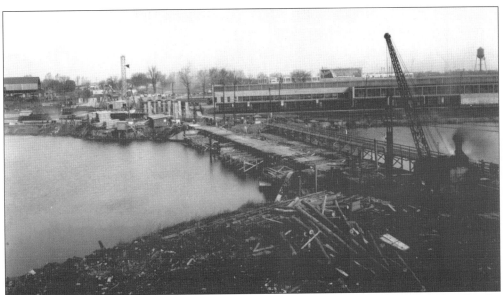

VIADUCT COLLAPSE. On the morning of Friday, April 12, 1929, the new cofferdam for the Logan Street (Martin Luther King Jr. Boulevard) viaduct collapsed, taking the lives of five workmen. Folwell Engineering Company of Chicago, the contractors for the construction, struggled to construct a new cofferdam to extricate the bodies of the victims. The five fatalities were Thomas Doertch, Henry Kramer, Fred Hock, Frank Harris, and Isaac Holman. William Carroll, a 20-year employee with Folwell, survived—as did Joseph Curtis, the only man to make it out of the cofferdam alive. (FPML/CADL.)

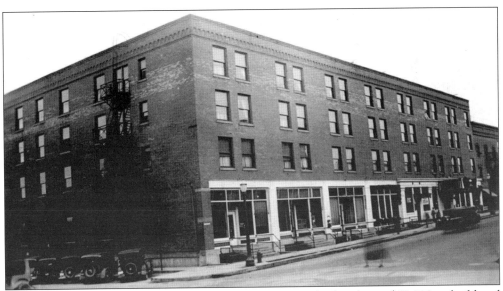

THE HOTEL KERNS. Built in 1909 by William G. Kerns, the hotel cost $50,000 to build and was the first hotel in the state of Michigan that had ice cold running water in every one of its 162 rooms. Located in the 100 block of North Grand Avenue, Kerns' location and the amenities that it offered made it popular with legislators and community groups. In January of 1922, the women's club Zonta held their first meeting at the Kerns. The Kerns also served as the bus station for the city of Lansing until 1932. (FPML/CADL.)

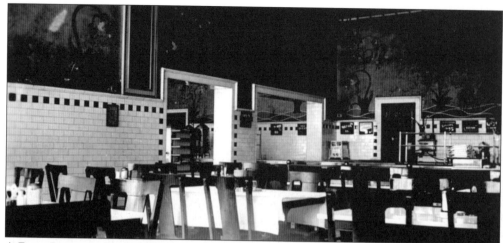

A Rare Interior Photograph of the Cafeteria in the Hotel Kerns. Known not only as a "fun place to stay" because of the rollicking bar at the hotel, the Kerns was also known for its popular cafeteria where busy workers and travelers could stop for a quick meal. (FPML/CADL.)

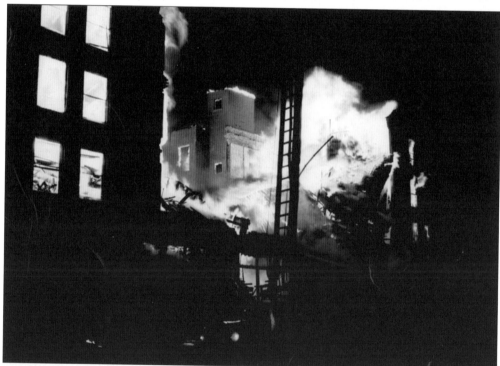

Hotel Kerns Fire. On December 11, 1934, a few minutes before 5:00 a.m., "Pop" Hayhoe, ". . . night janitor of the *State Journal*, . . . made his regular round through the editorial room of the newspaper's second floor, now empty of editors and reporters. Suddenly he stopped. A curl of flame licked up along some second floor window curtains on the hotel's north side, near the front. Before he could act the curl became a ravening sheet of flame. . . . Hayhoe wasted not an instant turning in the alarm. The Central fire station was only a block south of the hotel. His call completed, Hayhoe turned back. Window after window was ablaze. Now he could hear the screams of men and women, wakening to red horror!" From the *State Journal*. (FPML/CADL.)

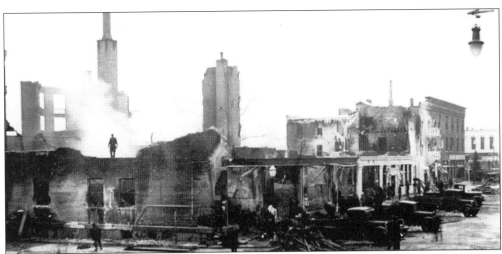

AFTERMATH, HOTEL KERNS FIRE. Hotel residents, forced out by the raging flames, leapt from the upper windows into the deployed fire nets, or were rescued by firemen who carried them down the ladders. For two hours firemen battled to prevent the blaze from breaching the firewall of the Hotel Wentworth. One fireman who was struck by a falling body worked for eight hours with a broken back. By 7:30 a.m. the fire was contained. Thirty-four people were killed in the fire; five of the bodies were never identified. The popular belief that people leapt from the Kerns and into the Grand River was dispelled by Captain Hugh Fisher who was present at the fire, and who stated in 1959 that no bodies were ever found in the Grand River. What caused the fire? A carelessly discarded cigarette. (FPML/CADL.)

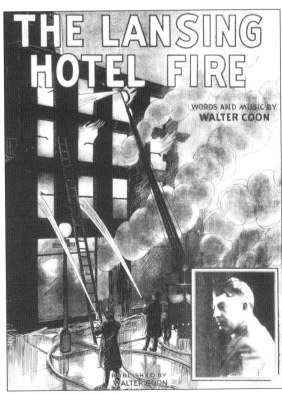

THE LANSING HOTEL FIRE, 1935. The Hotel Kerns fire moved Walter Coon of Royal Oak, Michigan, to write the words and music for his 1935 memorial song titled "The Lansing Hotel Fire." The first stanza recalls:

One evening when the stars up in heaven
Shone clear and bright o'er our land,
The city of Lansing in slumber
The hour of dawn was at hand,
The bell-boy shouted out fire
Tried hard to reach every one,
The sirens and cries, how they sounded
And the Kerns burning fast to the ground.

(Chorus)
We'll never forget the dear loved ones,
Bad luck seemed to be on their way,
The ones who had gone to that city,
Will rise to another new day.

117

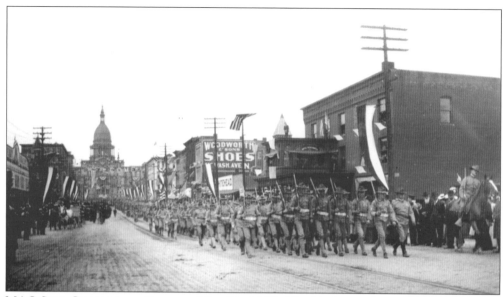

MAC SEMI-CENTENNIAL PARADE, MAY 31, 1907. The Michigan Agricultural College was also part of the Lansing community. From opening day in 1857 to the establishment of the Agricultural College post office in 1884, MAC was served by the Lansing post office. On May 31, 1907, President Theodore Roosevelt attended and addressed the citizens for the 50th anniversary of the founding of MAC. The capitol was adorned in patriotic splendor for the state's honored guest. A parade, complete with bands and military units, accompanied the President to the college.

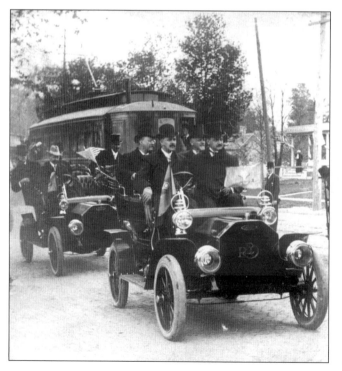

PRESIDENT ROOSEVELT & R.E. OLDS. Auto pioneer R.E. Olds had the pleasure of the President as his passenger in a new REO automobile on the trip to the college. In this historic photograph MAC President Jonathon L. Snyder and Roosevelt are seated in the rear of the car; R.E. Olds and Roosevelt's secretary, William Loeb, are seated in front. During this same year, East Lansing was incorporated as a city. In 1925, the college changed its name to Michigan State College. During the centennial in 1955, the college became known as Michigan State University.

Seven
RECREATION

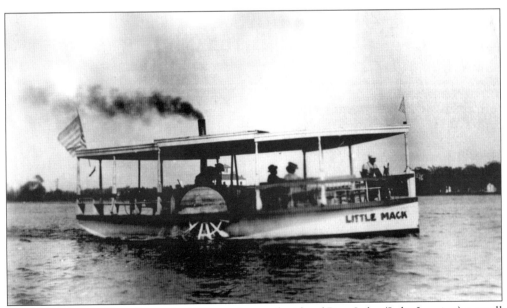

LITTLE MACK ON PINE LAKE. In 1870 on the north side of Pine Lake (Lake Lansing) a small rooming house was constructed. In 1874 the Lake House Hotel was built to accommodate the growing number of visitors to the lake. One of the easiest ways to reach the hotel was by steamer, and the *Little Mack* was one of the most popular steamers. In the center, just behind the *Little Mack*, you can see the Men's Clubhouse, which was known by a variety of names: Merry Sisters Club, Downey Club House, and the Izzer Club. The clubhouse was donated to the Lansing Sea Scouts and dismantled by the end of the 1930s. (Caterino/CADL.)

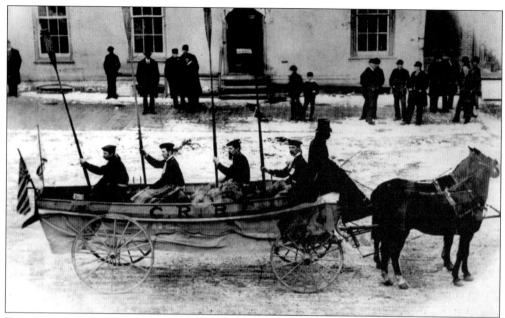

THE GRAND RIVER BOAT CLUB ON THE WAY TO ONE OF THEIR MEETS. Rowing in the late nineteenth century was a sport whose popularity would have rivaled that of professional football today. The rowers pictured are identified from back to front as Sam B. Taylor, Chas. A. Towne, George Cooper, and M.J. Buck. However, they have also been listed as, from back to front, Chas. A. Towne, George C. Cooper, Sam Taylor, and M.J. Buck in the bow. The club was formed in 1872 and dissolved in 1907. (FPML/CADL.)

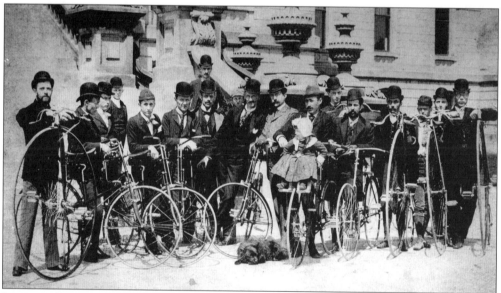

LANSING BICYCLE CLUB c. 1890. Notice the high and low bicycle types evident in this photograph. The bicyclists in this photograph from left to right are as follows: Edwyn Bowd, three unknown, Roy Jones (wearing cap), Ray Miller, O.A. Jenison, (behind Jenison) unknown, Lewis Waters, unknown, Burr Morgan, Morgan's daughter Grace, two unknown, Charles Humphrey, and Fred Moilliter. (FPML/CADL.)

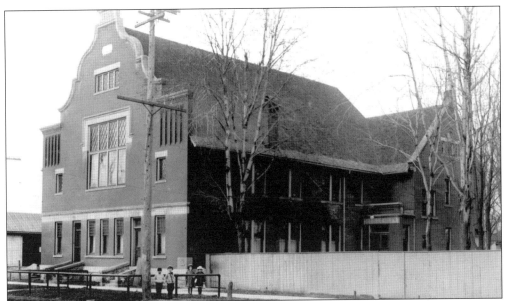

THE ARBEITER SOCIETY'S HALL LOCATED AT 608 NORTH GRAND AVENUE. The Arbeiter Society consisted of men of German descent and was famous for its band that played at a variety of Lansing civic functions. The hall was dedicated in 1905, the 30th anniversary of the club's founding. President Ernest Keller welcomed the visiting dignitaries while the choirs of Liederkranz and Arbeiter Societies sang "Das Deutsche Lied." (FPML/CADL.)

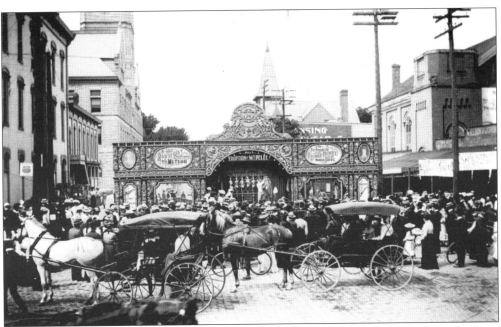

STREET FESTIVAL. In 1902, the Lansing Lodge 196 BPO Elks sponsored a street festival. Three shows were at this venue, "Alice Roosevelt christening the meteor, The Eruption of Mt Pelee, and The arrival of Price Henry to Washington D.C." It is unknown just what these shows were. The stage was set up in the 100 block of West Ottawa; notice the tower of the old City Hall to the left of the photo. (FPML/CADL.)

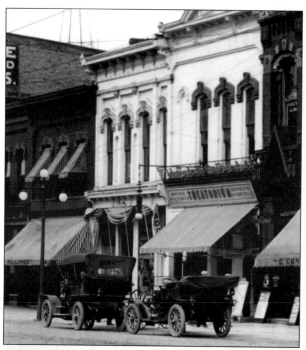

THE THEATORIUM WAS LOCATED AT 204 NORTH WASHINGTON AVENUE. It would later be known as the Capitol Theater and for a brief time in the late 1910s as the Empress. A theater operated on the site from 1910–1955. The number of theaters that once were in business in downtown Lansing is surprising; in 1921 there were nine theaters operating within a few blocks of each other. Today, not one of these theaters survives. (Caterino/CADL.)

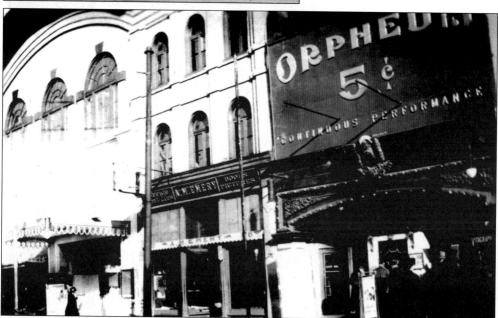

THE ORPHEUM THEATER. Constructed in 1910 at 114 North Washington, it was considered one of the finest theaters in the Midwest. Built by LeRoy Brown, the owner of the Vaudette Theater (122 North Washington), the Orpheum was promoted as being the finest 400-seat theater in the Midwest. Fuller Calfin designed the theater and no expense was spared to insure that it would be comfortable and luxurious. In 1914 Brown sold both the Orpheum and the Vaudette to E.C. Jarvis, who improved upon Brown's success by adding new innovations to enhance the patrons' experience. The Orpheum fell into decline in the late 1940s and closed in 1952, ignored and forgotten. (FPML/CADL.)

122

THE CAPITOL THEATER, 204 NORTH WASHINGTON AVENUE, 1921–1955. The first theater on this site was the Theatorium, which operated until the late 1910s when the business was sold to Joseph M. Neal, who renamed the theater the Empress. In 1921 the theater was sold to Claude E. Cady who renamed the theater the Capitol. The Dodge block, which housed the James O'Connor men's clothing store, is visible to the right in the photograph. (FPML/CADL.)

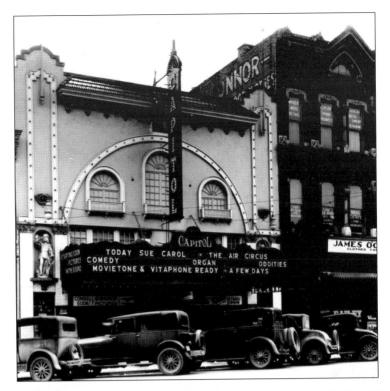

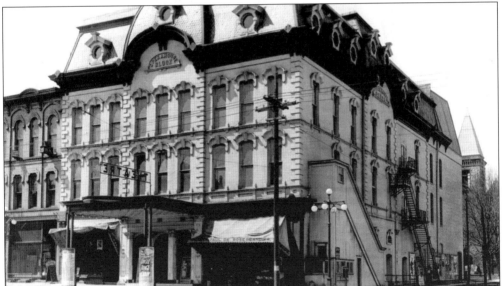

GLADMER THEATER. One of the finest of the Lansing theaters, the Gladmer began its life as Buck's Opera House in the 1870s. Designed by architect E.E. Myers, it was considered one of the finest theaters in Michigan. In 1890, Daniel Buck sold the theater to James Baird and it became know as Baird's Opera House. The theater remained Baird's Opera House until c. 1910, when it faced increasing competition from other downtown theaters. The decision was made that the theater needed to be remodeled. After an extensive modification, the theater was reopened and renamed the Gladmer. (FPML/CADL.)

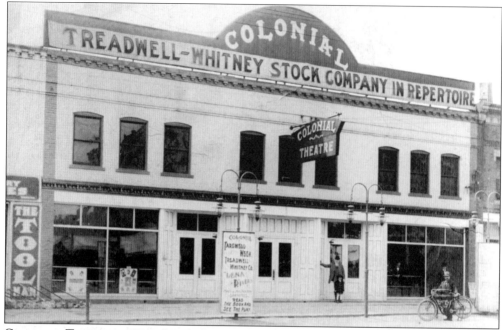

COLONIAL THEATER, 1911. Located at 122 East Michigan Avenue, the Colonial Theater began life in 1900. In the 1930s, the theater's name was changed by its new owner, the Butterfield Company, to the Lansing Theater. The Butterfield Company operated it until 1953, when it was known in its final reincarnation as the Esquire Theater. Today the site is a parking lot. To the right in the photograph is a motorcycle, just what type is unknown. Headlining at the theater was the play Lena Rivers presented by the Treadwell-Whitney Company.

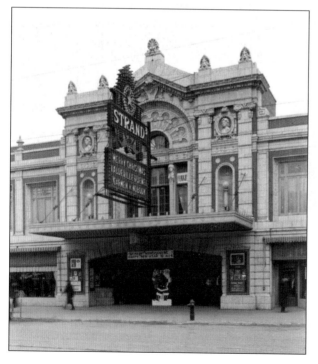

STRAND THEATER, C. 1920s. The Strand Theater began as the project of Walter S. Butterfield, who wanted to build one of the finest theaters in Michigan. Ground was broken in March of 1920 and the building was completed in April of 1921. The theater had a seating capacity of 1,786, and the site also housed a bowling alley, a billiard room, and a banquet hall. The Strand Theater remained popular with movie-going patrons. The building began to display its age and in 1941 the theater was remodeled in an Art Deco style. The old marquee was replaced with a new one, introducing it under the theater's new name, the Michigan Theater. (Caterino/CADL.)

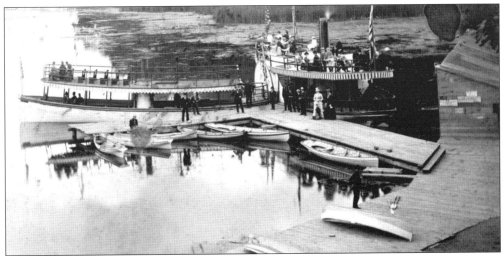

BOARDING THE RIVERBOATS FOR LEADLEY PARK, C. 1898. Patrons boarded the boats at the Logan Street dock and cruised upriver to the park, which was located at what is now Waverly and the Grand River. Leadley Park would later add a hotel and roller coaster and competed quite well with the resort at Pine Lake. (FPML/CADL.)

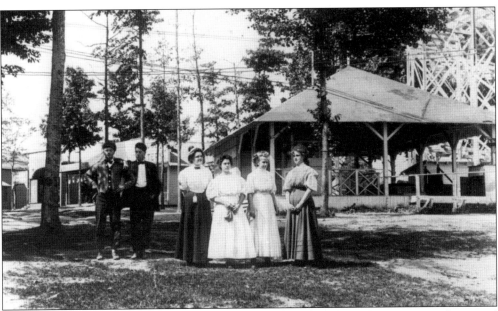

AN OUTING FOR THE DAY AT WAVERLY PARK, C. 1905. Waverly Park, originally named Leadley Park after Gottlieb Leadley, its owner, was immediately popular with the people of Lansing. The park opened on July 4, 1892 to huge crowds who stayed well into the evening hours. Tragically, Leadley would die in 1897 and the park was sold in 1903 to the Lansing City Electric Railroad Company. The following year its name was changed to Waverly Park and the now-named Lansing and Suburban Traction Company began adding attractions to the park. It was not uncommon for streetcar companies to own amusement parks as a way to generate an increase in fares on the weekends when ridership was down. The park closed in 1917, a victim of the growing popularity of the Pine Lake Park. The park's popular roller coaster is visible at right. To the left is the entrance to the park's midway. (FPML/CADL.)

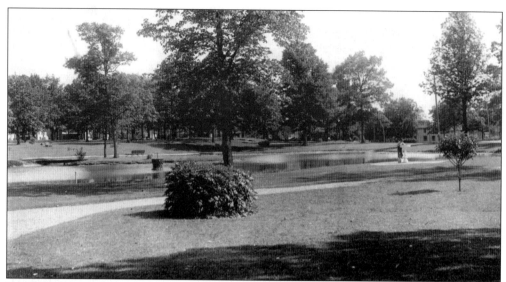

EAST SIDE PARK, NOW OAK PARK. The park covered 20 acres and the lake was one acre in circumference with a quarter-acre island in the center. A rustic bridge connected it to the shore. The lake was filled in some time in the 1950s. In the background, Prudden Wheel Plant is visible. Prior to becoming a park, the site served as one of Lansing's earliest cemeteries. (FPML/CADL.)

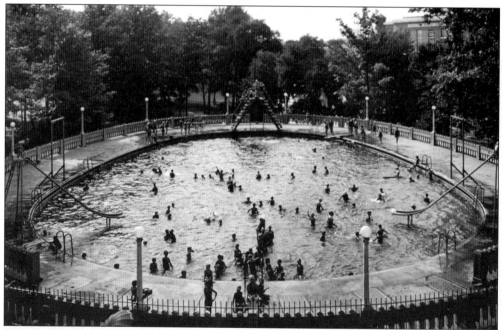

SUMMERTIME FUN. The Moores Park Pool is one of the few remaining Wesley Bintz-designed pools in the country. Wesley Bintz came to Lansing from Flint in 1920 to serve as a structural engineer with the city engineer's office. Under his direction the Moores Park Pool was built, as well as five bridges: Elm Street, Main Street, Saginaw Street, Seymour Street and Shiawassee Street. After 1923, he decided to design pools full-time and began the Bintz Pool Company. The most unique feature of a Bintz pool was the incorporation of the changing rooms into the pool's structure. The Moores Park Pool was added to the National Register of Historic Places in 1985. (FPML/CADL.)

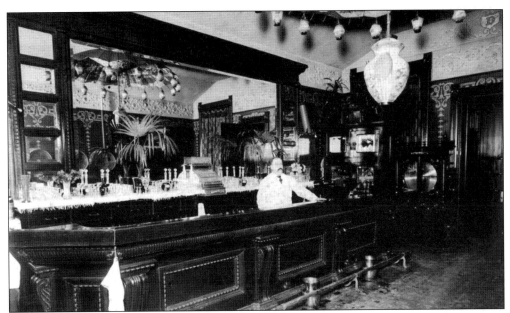

THE DOWNEY HOTEL BARTENDER, RICHARD WAITE, IN 1904. This is a wonderful picture of the most famous watering hole in Lansing. Most major political officials conducted business at the Downey; it was the place to go after a hard day at the office. Notice the unique chandelier and the spittoons alongside the bar. Richard Waite, Dick to his friends, kept a neat and clean establishment. It appears odd that there are no beer taps. (FPML/CADL.)

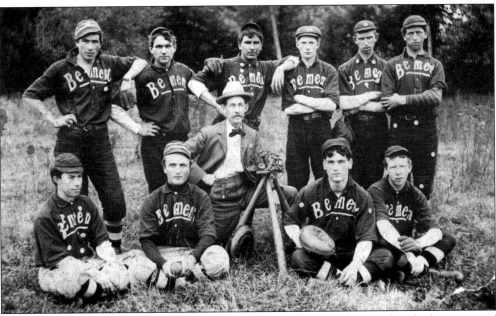

THE BEMENT BASEBALL TEAM, C. 1890S. The team's record is unknown, but the last names of many of the players are known. Pictured from left to right are the following: (standing) Martin Eggert, Massuck, Stodul (?), Fraser, Schmidt, and Buff Murphy, (sitting) Mac Skoranski, Frisbie, Bugbee, Hurtel, and unknown. It is interesting to note that there were only ten players on the team so, unlike today, many of the players had to learn to play multiple positions. (FPML/CADL.)

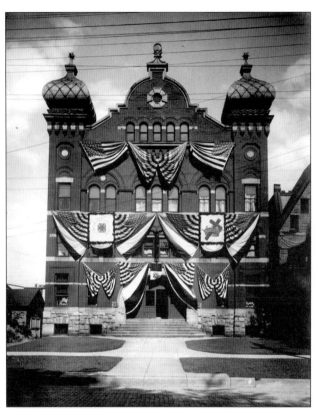

THE MASONIC TEMPLE OF LANSING LOCATED AT 213 SOUTH CAPITOL AVENUE. The cornerstone for this building was laid in 1901 and the building was dedicated in 1905. The temple was built of red brick and is 147 feet deep and 32 feet wide. Contained within were an auditorium, clubrooms, a library, dining room, and kitchen. The growth of the Masonic groups in Lansing required a large structure and the new temple was built next door in 1927. The old temple building then served as the Veterans Memorial Building. (FPML/CADL.)

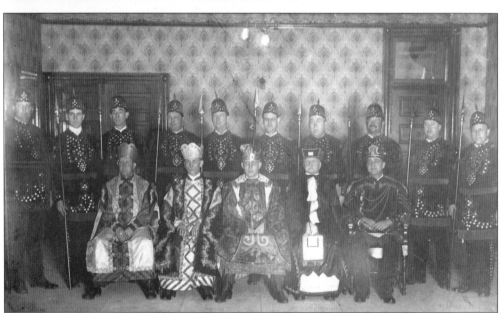

THE LANSING LODGE LOYAL ORDER OF THE MOOSE #288 IN 1914. This image is one of the heavy weight degree team whose ceremonial robes were at the time considered the finest in the state. The chief steward of the lodge was Charles H. Williams, and the lodge was located at 106 West Shiawassee Street. (FPML/CADL).